LABOUR MANAGEMENT RELATIONS SERIES

labour-
management
relations
series
n° 48

Workers' Participation
in decisions
within undertakings

Summary of Discussions of a
Symposium on Workers' Participation in
Decisions within Undertakings
(Oslo, 20-30 August 1974)

Geneva
International Labour Office

532709

ISBN 92-2-101452-5

First published 1976

HD
5650
.I8
1976

The designations employed in ILO publications, which are in conformity with United Nations practice, and the presentation of material therein do not imply the expression of any opinion whatsoever on the part of the International Labour Office concerning the legal status of any country or territory or of its authorities, or concerning the delimitation of its frontiers.

The responsibility for opinions expressed in signed articles, studies and other contributions rests solely with their authors, and publication does not constitute an endorsement by the International Labour Office of the opinions expressed in them.

ILO publications can be obtained through major booksellers or ILO local offices in many countries, or direct from ILO Publications, International Labour Office, CH-1211 Geneva 22, Switzerland. A catalogue or list of new publications will be sent free of charge from the above address.

TABLE OF CONTENTS

PREFACE

In accordance with a decision taken by the Governing Body of the ILO at its 190th Session (May-June 1973), a Symposium on Workers' Participation in Decisions within Undertakings organised by the ILO in collaboration with the Norwegian Government, was convened in Oslo from 20 to 30 August 1974.

This Symposium was a follow-up of two previous ILO meetings which had dealt with workers' participation at the enterprise level, namely, the Technial Meeting on the Rights of Trade Union Representatives and Participation of Workers in Decisions within Undertakings, held in Geneva in 1967[1], and an International Seminar on Workers' Participation in Decisions within Undertakings held in Belgrade in 1969.[2] The International Institute for Labour Studies has, during the past few years, published a series of national monographs on workers' participation in management, within the framework of a comparative research project.[3]

No rigid agenda was fixed for the Symposium, but the Governing Body decided that its discussions should centre on two main issues:

(a)   institutional arrangements by which workers' representatives are associated with various decisions (e.g. collective bargaining, joint consultation, worker members of managerial bodies); and

(b)   arrangements for associating workers with the determination of work organisation at the shop-floor level.

The Symposium was not intended to adopt any policy recommendations for future ILO action; it was designed to provide an opportunity to assess the rapid developments that have taken place in recent years in the field of workers' participation and to permit a broad exchange of views and experience, with particular emphasis on workers' participation at the level of the shop floor and workplace.

All the States Members of the ILO were invited to send participants, drawn from government, employers', workers' or

----

[1] The documents of this meeting have been reproduced in ILO, Labour-Management Relations Series No. 33 (Geneva, 1969).

[2] The documents of this meeting have been published in document ILO/TAP/R.23 (Geneva, 1970).

[3] Cf. International Institute for Labour Studies, National Monographs on India and Poland in Bulletin No. 5, November 1968; on France, the Federal Republic of Germany and the United States in Bulletin No. 6, June 1969; on Israel, Japan and Spain in Bulletin No. 7, June 1970; on Yugoslavia and Great Britain in Bulletin No. 9, 1972. The Institute also published (mimeographed) a national monograph on the Netherlands in 1971 (ref. WPM 12) and an appendix, by K.N. Vaid, entitled "Further data on the operation of workers' participation in management in India" (ref. WPM 4 (App.) 1970). An updated issue of its "Workers' participation in management" selected bibliography 1950-1970, published in 1971, is under preparation.

academic circles. A total of 176 participants from 51 countries and 23 observers attended the Symposium and took part in the discussions.

The background paper reproduced below was prepared by the International Labour Office to provide the participants with a general picture of the principal forms of workers' participation which are applied in practice or are under discussion in various parts of the world today, emphasising in particular the developments which have occurred in the past few years. A large number of written contributions were submitted by the participants, describing the experience with various systems of participation in different countries, the list of which is appended to this report (Appendix III). This volume also includes a brief report of the discussions relating to specific aspects of the subject, as well as the summing-up of the main issues and trends which emerged from the discussions at the Symposium as a whole, delivered orally by Mr. J. Schregle, Chief of the Labour Law and Labour Relations Branch of the ILO, at the final session.

BACKGROUND PAPER

Prepared by
the International Labour Office

I. INSTITUTIONAL ARRANGEMENTS FOR PARTICIPATION OF
    WORKERS' REPRESENTATIVES IN DECISIONS

1. Workers' management of under-
    takings and related systems

From a conceptual viewpoint, workers' management of undertakings or self-management represents the most far-reaching degree of association of workers in decisions concerning them.

Probably the best known example of this type of workers' participation is the Yugoslav system of self-management which has been the subject of a large number of studies and publications and has some twenty years' experience.[1] Under the Yugoslav system, the workforce of the undertaking exercises the principal functions of management through the self-management organs, the organisation and powers of which have been established since the sixties by the statute or internal regulations of the undertaking, namely, the workers' assembly and the workers' council. The latter is elected by secret ballot by the personnel from among its members, usually for a term of two years, at the end of which its members are not immediately eligible for re-election, in order to ensure rotation of membership. The workers' council enjoys wide powers in the field of management in general; for example, it adopts the internal regulations (including those concerning distribution of income), development plans and other programmes of the undertaking, supervises their implementation, decides on investments and approves the balance sheet. Every four years, it elects the director of the undertaking, whom it is also empowered to dismiss, and it generally sets up a management board and a supervisory committee, as well as a whole series of specialised committees to which are delegated advisory or decision-making powers in specific fields (for example, recruitment and dismissal of certain categories of employees, grievances, planning, financial and commercial affairs, etc.). Important matters such as mergers or the conversion of the undertaking may be, in general, submitted to a referendum of the personnel, but in practice, decisions on these matters are usually taken by the workers' assembly.

This system of self-management, introduced in 1950 after a period of highly centralised management and planning, was extended after 1953 to so-called non-economic activities (education, administration, health and social security services, etc.). Since 1971, a great many efforts have been made to carry out a thorough renovation of the system and to remedy certain difficulties to which even the highest authorities in the country have drawn attention.

----

[1] Cf. for example, International Labour Office, Studies and Reports, New Series 64, Workers' management in Yugoslavia, Geneva 1962, 320 pp.

In this perspective, a Workers' Self-Management Congress, organised by the trade unions, was held in Sarajevo in May 1971, which adopted almost thirty important resolutions. Among the twenty-one constitutional amendments adopted the following month by the Federal Assembly, those which dealt directly with self-management of undertakings gave constitutional sanction to the recommendations of this Congress relating, among other things to the policy of distribution of income and to the total application of the principle of direct self-management by the workers in the basic work units, in order to avoid a situation where the workers participated less and less directly in self-management. These principles have been incorporated in the new Federal Constitution of Yugoslavia promulgated at the beginning of 1974. Thus, at the present time, while on the one hand the autonomy of undertakings has been reinforced, on the other hand self-management is being decentralised through the operation of self-management organs at two or, in the case of large enterprises, three different levels, namely, at the level of the undertaking as a whole, at the level of its economic units (plants or establishments) and at the level of its work units (shops or departments, etc.). The shop-floor assemblies, which constitute the basic self-management organs, are empowered, for example, to adopt production plans and works rules for the unit, as well as deciding upon the distribution of income among the workers, taking account of the principles of distribution established by the workers' council and of the legal minimum. They may also delegate certain of their functions to the executive committee elected by their members.

Parallel with efforts to stabilise the economy, a Code for worker-managers has been drafted, designed to specify their rights and duties as well as the basic ethical principles of self-management.

In Algeria, management boards composed of workers appeared at the time of accession to independence, after the departure of most of the owners and managers of the industrial and agricultural undertakings. These boards were recognised by the Decrees of March 1963, and they very soon evolved into a system of self-management which was progressively replaced, in subsequent years, especially in the industrial sector, by centralised state management. Since 1965 the Algerian Government has pursued a policy of promoting workers to become producer-managers and in 1971 a Charter and a Code of socialist management of undertakings was adopted. For non-agricultural public undertakings subject to this Code, it provides for the election, for a three-year term, of unit assemblies, which act as trade union councils, and undertaking assemblies of from seven to twenty-five members, elected by these unit assemblies. These assemblies are empowered to assist in the definition of the general policy of the undertaking by issuing opinions and recommendations on the budget estimates of the undertaking, as well as on draft programmes, including investment plans. They are called upon to supervise the management of the undertaking and to approve the balance sheet and the operating accounts. They are also obliged to assist the management in the establishment of personnel policies, particularly as regards recruitment, dismissals, training, health and safety and the improvement of working conditions. They are in charge of welfare services. Specialised permanent committees (from one to five) are provided for to deal with economic and financial matters, social and cultural matters, personnel and training, and - in committees which include an equal number of management representatives - disciplinary matters and safety and health. The management is expected to speak with one voice, in order to maintain a co-ordinated administration of the undertaking, while at the same time having a collegiate structure. Under the authority of the director, the management board includes the main supervisory staff as well as one or two representatives of the personnel elected by the workers' assembly. The management board is obliged to attend the meetings of the workers' assembly in an advisory capacity.

This new system has already been applied experimentally for some time and has been the object of a broad national campaign to explain its purpose and functions. However, the election of the assemblies, which was to take place in 1973 in a certain number of undertakings, had to be postponed until the beginning of 1974.

In Peru, the Government has decided to apply a system of self-management in a sector known as "social property", which receives an initial aid from the State, and which is expected to cover more than a thousand undertakings in the coming years.

A self-management system, which is rarely so-called, although the workers exercise a direct influence on the management of their undertaking, is the system of producers' co-operatives which is found in a certain number of industrialised countries and various developing countries, in agriculture as well as in industry and the service sector. The members of authentic producers' co-operative are in fact workers, owners and managers of the undertaking, which is managed by a board and management staff, elected or appointed by them. A variety of different types of such co-operatives exists and in certain countries they have close links with the State.

Finally, cases have occurred in the past few months, in France and in the United Kingdom, in particular, where the personnel of an undertaking has applied systems inspired by principles of self-defence, if not of self-management, in connection with "active strikes", involving the occupation of the undertaking when it was about to close as a result of serious economic difficulties. The Lip affair in France is one example which attracted particular publicity. In similar circumstances, undertakings have sometimes been transformed into producers' co-operatives.

2. Participation of workers' representatives in management organs

For varying lengths of time, in a large number of countries, and by virtue in most cases of a legal obligation, workers' representatives have been included in management organs in the public sector as a whole or in certain nationalised undertakings, or again in the railways, national airways, or various public services such as posts and telecommunications, gas, water and electricity services, etc. This is the case, for example, in Argentina, Australia, Austria, Belgium, Egypt (where equal representation was introduced in 1963), France, Ghana, India, Ireland, Israel, Italy, Mali, Mexico, Nigeria, Norway, Peru, Sri Lanka, Switzerland, Syria, Tanzania, the United Kingdom and Venezuela. The Government of Bangladesh has undertaken recently the study of a system of workers' representation in management organs of undertakings in the public sector. In this connection, the growing importance of public undertakings in the industry of many developing countries should be underlined.

These workers' representatives may be directly nominated by
the trade unions, or by the government on the proposal of the trade
unions, or elected by the personnel. Their number and influence
vary a great deal from one country to another and from one
undertaking to another, by reason of the functions entrusted to them
by law or in practice, and because of their standard of education
and training for this role.

In the private sector, the system which has pushed workers'
representation to the furthest degree is that of co-determination
applied in the Federal Republic of Germany since the beginning of
the fifties. This system has been the object of numerous studies
and has attracted special attention in many countries. By an Act of
1951, equal representation of workers was established on the
supervisory boards of large iron and steel and mining undertakings.
These boards generally include five workers' representatives (one
worker and one salaried employee nominated by the works council from
among members of the personnel of the undertaking, and three
representatives nominated by the trade union organisations, one of
whom must come from outside the undertaking and the said
organisations), five representatives of the shareholders, and an
eleventh member nominated by mutual agreement. In addition, one of
the members of the directorate or management board (appointed by the
supervisory board) namely, the "labour director" who is generally
responsible for personnel questions and social affairs, may only be
nominated or dismissed in agreement with the majority of the
workers' members of that board.

Under an Act of 1952, the workers' representation on the
supervisory boards of companies which do not belong to the above
industries is only one-third of the total membership. For some time
and with increasing insistence in recent years, the German
Confederation of Trade Unions has been demanding equal
representation of workers on the supervisory boards of companies in
sectors other than iron and steel and mining, at least for
undertakings of a certain size or with a certain financial turnover.
This demand has met with strong opposition on the part of the German
Employers' Confederation, which has seen in it, among other things,
an attack on property rights as well as a threat to the market
economy, to the autonomy of the parties in collective bargaining and
to the efficiency of management. The present coalition government
of the Social Democratic and Liberal Parties has reached agreement
on the principles of new legislation on this subject, which is in
preparation.

In several other Western European countries, legislation has
been drafted or adopted during the past few years with a view to
introducing workers' representation in management organs of private
undertakings, or to reinforcing existing representation, but in most
cases workers have only been granted a minority representation as
compared to that of shareholders.

In Austria, an Act adopted at the end of 1973 brought up to
one-third the representation of workers elected by the works council
to the supervisory board, in companies with a certain level of
capital assets, whereas previously workers only had two
representatives on such boards.

In Denmark, an Act was adopted a little earlier allowing
workers two representatives on boards of directors and a Bill was
introduced in Parliament at the beginning of 1973 with a view to

creating a national investment fund, constituted by a levy on employers, both public and private, calculated as a certain percentage of wages, which, among other things, would allow workers to have a number of representatives on each board corresponding to their share of the capital of the undertaking, up to a maximum of 50 per cent.

In France, an Act of 1972 brought up to four members, one of whom represents the foremen and one the graduate engineers and other supervisory staff, the works committee delegation which participates in an advisory capacity in the management board of joint stock companies under the previous legislation. Some of these joint stock companies with a management board and a supervisory board, which were instituted under an Act of 1966, include in their supervisory board representatives of the personnel, who have the same rights as the shareholders' representatives, and the Government is considering the generalisation of this formula for companies which adopt such a structure.

In Luxembourg, the Government introduced a Bill in April 1973, which envisages, among other things, the introduction of workers' representatives in a proportion of at least one-third in the management boards of companies employing at least 1,000 workers.

In Norway, an Act which came into force in 1973 provides for the establishment, in mining and manufacturing undertakings which employ more than 200 workers, of a new type of assembly of which a third of the members are to be elected by the personnel. This assembly has the final power of decision concerning important investments as well as in matters of rationalisation or reorganisation of the undertaking which substantially affect the employees. It nominates the board of directors, on a basis of proportional representation if one-third of its members require this, which may result in the nomination of one-third (at least two) of the members of the board by the workers' representatives. Companies in the extractive or manufacturing industries which employ from 51 to 199 workers are obliged, if the majority of the workers so requests, to hold an election by the personnel of a maximum of one-third and no less than two of the members of their boards of directors. A similar system was introduced by the Government a few months ago in the construction industry, after having been the subject of a prior joint agreement. Another joint agreement introduced experimentally for the period 1974-75 a formula adapted to newspaper publishing undertakings. The Norwegian authorities are also envisaging rulings of this type applicable to hotels and the catering industry and transportation from 1975 onwards, and they are studying the application of such systems in commercial and agricultural undertakings, co-operatives, banks, insurance companies and state-owned companies.

In the Netherlands, an Act which came into force in 1973 provides for the introduction, in companies employing more than 100 persons and possessing a certain amount of capital assets, of a new method of appointment by co-optation of the members of supervisory boards - which henceforth are empowered to appoint the managers - with the works council having veto rights. The objective, in this case, is to enable the members of the board to enjoy the confidence of the workers as well as of the shareholders. In case of a veto, the board may appeal to the national tripartite Economic and Social Council, which has the final right of decision.

In the United Kingdom, the trade union movement published in 1973 a report requesting joint representation of workers, to be chosen from among trade union representatives, in an organ of the supervisory board type, in private as well as nationalised undertakings, with similar arrangements for public services. This board would have veto rights over the management and the general assembly of shareholders with regard to important decisions (closing down of plants, mergers, investments of a certain size, etc.). The British employers' organisations, while favouring an extension of workers' participation in decisions within undertakings, in particular through joint consultation procedures, have taken a stand in opposition to the participation system proposed by the workers' organisation.

In Sweden, under an Act of December 1972, all limited companies employing at least 100 persons, except insurance companies and banks, are obliged, if the trade union delegates in the undertaking so require, to admit two representatives of their employees nominated by the local trade union to sit on their board of directors. These representatives may, however, not take part in discussions concerning a labour dispute or in negotiations which may result in a collective agreement.

In Switzerland, the trade unions launched a proposal in 1971 with a view to endowing the Confederation with "the right to legislate concerning the participation of workers and their organisations in decisions within undertakings and administrations". This question will eventually be settled by a popular vote, but in the meantime a lively debate is taking place concerning such participation, which might involve workers' representation on boards of directors.

A number of national trade union federations and the international trade union organisations are concerned to promote the development of workers' participation in decisions in multinational companies, in one form or another. With regard to Western Europe, the Commission of the European Communities submitted to the Council of Ministers in 1970 a draft statute for a European company which contains provisions comparable in some respects to the system applied in the Federal Republic of Germany. The supervisory board, which would include only a proportion of one-third of workers' representatives, elected by the members of existing representative organs in the various plants at the national level, would be empowered to give prior authorisation for the decisions of the management board concerning the closing down or the transfer of the undertaking or of large sections of it, substantial restrictions or extensions of its activities, important changes in its organisation, and co-operation with other undertakings. In 1972, the Commission prepared a proposal for a Vth Directive, with a view to the harmonisation of the laws governing joint stock companies in its member States, which included provisions for a similar system of workers' participation in the nomination of the members of supervisory boards in companies employing at least 500 workers, either according to a formula similar to that in effect in the Federal Republic of Germany (nomination in the proportion of at least one third by the employees or their representatives or on their proposal) or according to a method comparable to that in force at the present time in the Netherlands. However, the principle of participation by workers in management organs, even on a minority basis, does not meet with unanimous agreement within the European Community either in employers' circles or among the trade unions.

Outside Europe, workers' participation in management organs in the private sector seems to have been developed, up to the present, to a lesser degree. In <u>Algeria</u>, the part of the Code of socialist management of undertakings which applies to this sector provides for two officers of the trade union section in the undertaking to be present at meetings of the board of management or administration. In <u>Libya</u>, under recent legislation, two workers' representatives are included in management boards. In <u>Pakistan</u>, an Ordinance of 1972, revised by an Act of 1973, provided that, in undertakings with 50 or more workers, one-fifth of the members of the management should be representatives of the personnel, nominated by the trade union which is recognised by the management for collective bargaining purposes, or, failing this, elected by the workers. In any case, the management must include at least one such representative. A written opinion from these representatives is required before any decision may be taken concerning promotion policy and works' rules or discipline, changes in working conditions, training on the job and welfare. The employer is obliged to reply to such an opinion within a specified time and if no agreement is reached the matter is subject to collective bargaining. In <u>Peru</u>, since 1970, "industrial communities" of a co-operative type have been set up in every private enterprise employing at least six full-time workers, for the purpose of managing part of the funds arising out of the system of profit sharing. These organs must have at least one representative on the management board, the number of representatives increasing with their share of the capital up to a limit of 50 per cent.

3. <u>Works councils, works committees, joint consultation bodies and similar institutions for workers' representation</u>

Works councils or works committees, or again joint consultation bodies, remain by far the commonest form of machinery for workers' participation in decisions within undertakings in both industrialised and developing countries.

In many countries these bodies have been set up by legislation, e.g. <u>Austria</u>, <u>Belgium</u>, <u>Burma</u>, <u>Burundi</u>, <u>Finland</u>, <u>France</u>, <u>Federal Republic of Germany</u>, <u>Indonesia</u>, <u>Iraq</u>, <u>Luxembourg</u>, the <u>Netherlands</u>, <u>Pakistan</u>, <u>Spain</u>, <u>Sri Lanka</u>, <u>Tanzania</u>, <u>Tunisia</u>, <u>Zaire</u> and <u>Zambia</u>.[1] In some cases (for example, in <u>Indonesia</u>) the setting up of these organs is only compulsory in public undertakings. In other countries such as <u>Denmark</u>, <u>Norway</u> and <u>Sweden</u>, they have been established by agreements concluded between the central workers' and employers' organisations. In certain countries, again, they have been instituted not by national agreements but through collective agreements concluded for certain industries or directly between the management of an undertaking and the workers represented by their trade unions, or at the initiative of the employer, on a purely voluntary basis. This type of system is found, for example, in <u>Australia</u>, <u>Canada</u>, <u>Ireland</u>, <u>Japan</u>, <u>New Zealand</u>, <u>Portugal</u>,

[1] The institution of trade union committees, which is also provided for by law in the USSR and the other Eastern European countries, will be dealt with under a different heading, below, since their role is not strictly comparable to that of works councils or committees in countries with a market economy.

Switzerland and the United Kingdom, as well as in several developing countries, in particular in Cyprus, India, Indonesia, Malaysia, Singapore and in a number of English-speaking African countries.

In most countries, these bodies have a joint composition, including both representatives of the personnel and representatives of the management, quite often on an equal basis. In others - for example in Austria and the Federal Republic of Germany - they are composed only of representatives of the workers. The workers' representatives in works councils or works committees are often elected either by the employees as a whole or only by the workers who are members of the trade union, unless they are nominated directly by the union. In some cases the unions enjoy the exclusive right of nominating candidates (in Belgium, for example) or have priority in this respect, as is the case, in particular, in Finland, France and Tunisia. Even in the countries, such as Austria, and the Federal Republic of Germany, where the legislation does not generally grant such privileges to the trade unions, the great majority of the members of works councils are trade unionists.

Great diversity is also evident in the attributions of the works councils or works committees, which generally deal with clearly specified matters. Their field of competence ranges from mere receipt of information (in particular on the general economic and financial situation of the undertaking and its prospects), often followed by consultation on a variety of subjects, to the right of co-decision, mainly concerning personnel matters and working conditions. In addition, they are often entrusted with the management of welfare services. In the majority of cases, their attributions have been clearly defined to distinguish them from matters which are subject to collective bargaining between employers and trade unions.

Several countries of Western Europe - Austria, Belgium, France, the Federal Republic of Germany and the Netherlands - have enlarged the scope of competence of their works councils, in particular through legislation adopted during recent years, but sometimes also by collective agreement.

In the main, in Austria, the Federal Republic of Germany and the Netherlands, the trend has been towards extension of the information to be given to the works councils concerning the economic and financial situation of the undertaking to include forecasts such as investment programmes, plans for rationalisation and the introduction of new methods or processes, the reduction of production and changes in the structure of the undertaking (closing down or transfer, in whole or in part, mergers, etc.), thus including generally forecasts which may entail substantial changes in the employment situation or pattern and working conditions. In most cases, this right to information is henceforth accompanied by the right to consultation at the planning stage; the employer is generally obliged to indicate the measures he intends to take to avoid or lessen any unfavourable consequences for the workers, and the works council is empowered, for its part, to discuss these forecasts and proposals and to suggest other solutions.

In Belgium, where a Royal Decree of 27 November 1973 issued regulations concerning the economic and financial information to be supplied to works councils, under the terms of national agreements concluded some years ago, the head of the undertaking is obliged, on

request from the workers' delegates, to inform the works council   of
the   rules   in   operation   concerning   personnel policy, applying in
particular to recruitment, selection, transfers and promotion.   The
works   council   is empowered to determine, on a proposal by the head
of undertaking or the workers' delegates, the general criteria to be
followed in case   of   redundancy   or   re-employment   resulting   from
economic or technical circumstances.

In   France, the works committees play an increased role in the
participation of the personnel in profits, which was   instituted   by
an   Ordinance   of   1967.   In addition, under the terms of a national
agreement of 1969 on job   security,   they   must   be   consulted   when
collective   dismissals   are envisaged for economic reasons.   The Act
concerning continuous vocational training, adopted   in   1971,   also
makes   their   consultation   compulsory on a certain number of points
relating to   such   training.   Finally,   an   Act   of   December   1973
entrusted   to   them   new   attributions in the field of conditions of
work and provided that a specialised committee be set   up   for   this
purpose in enterprises with 300 or more employees.

As   regards   the right of co-decision[1], in the Netherlands, an
Act of 1971, which replaced that of 1950 concerning   works   councils
requires   not   only consultation with these organs but their consent
before any decision may be   taken   relating   in   particular   to   the
establishment   or   change   of   work schedules or holiday arrangements
and any safety or hygiene measures.   An Act adopted in January 1972,
in the Federal Republic of Germany, extended the already substantial
list of questions on which decisions must be taken   jointly   by   the
employers   and   the   works councils, including, among other matters,
the determination of standards for piecework and incentive payments.
Co-decision is also obligatory henceforth for directives   concerning
the selection of personnel in connection with recruitment, transfers
or changes of grade.

The Austrian Acts adopted in 1971 and 1973 also   enlarged   the
rights   of co-decision of the works councils.   Since 1971, incentive
payments and bonuses may only be fixed with   the   agreement   of   the
works   council,   in cases where they are not included in collective
agreements.   The same is true for work schedules and   rest   periods.
The   1973 Act laid down in even greater detail the list of functions
of works councils and the areas where a right of co-decision may   be
required   concerning   works   rules   and   those   where   these   may be
established by agreement.

In Luxembourg, the Bill mentioned above provided   for   the
setting   up   of   joint committees, in private undertakings with more
than 250 employees, which would have the power of   deciding   on   the
establishment   or   modification   of   general criteria for selection,
evaluation, transfer, promotion or dismissal of workers.

Under the draft statute for a European   company,   prepared   by
the   European Communities, there would be a European works committee
which would be kept informed regularly by the   management   board   on
the general economic situation of the company, its prospects for the
----

[1] In   Austria,   the   Federal Republic of Germany and the
Netherlands, where the management and the works council   are   unable
to   reach   the   required   agreement,   the   matter is submitted to an
arbitration body.

future and the effects on employment, and its investment programme. In addition, the management board would not be empowered to take decisions without the agreement of the European works committee on matters concerning: principles governing recruitment, promotion and dismissals; the carrying out of vocational training; the principles governing wages and the introduction of new methods of remuneration; health and safety measures; the setting up and administration of welfare services; the times for starting and stopping work; and the establishment of holiday schedules. Where agreement could not be reached, the matter could be decided by an ad hoc arbitration body.

Among the developing countries, special mention may be made of Algeria, Tanzania and Zambia which have recently adopted legislation setting up works councils or similar organs with wide powers. In Algeria, by virtue of the provisions of the Code of socialist management of undertakings applicable to the private sector, the officers of the trade union section of the enterprise or unit have responsibility, in particular, in addition to negotiating the collective agreement for the undertaking or plant, for proposing any measures which might improve productivity, expressing an opinion on the investment programme and the balance sheet, presenting personnel grievances to the employer, orienting and supervising training, nominating workers' representatives on joint committees for safety and health and discipline, and administering welfare services.

In Tanzania, by a presidential circular issued in 1970, workers' councils were added to the existing works committees in public and parastatal undertakings employing more than ten persons. These councils, one-fourth of the members of which are workers' representatives, provide advice on the application in the undertaking of the Government's wages and incomes policy as well as on the undertakings' production, organisational and marketing programmes. They also examine the balance sheet. The executive committee, which includes a maximum of one-third workers' representatives among its members, elected by the workers' council, is empowered to examine such matters, as well as financial plans, and to give advice on the general policy suggested by the workers' council and the current management and, in general, acts as an adviser to the manager of the undertaking.

In Zambia, an Act of 1971, which has not yet officially come into force, provided among other things for the setting up of works councils in undertakings with more than 100 employees. These councils are entitled to receive information concerning decisions of an economic and financial nature, job evaluation and the wage system. They have the right to be consulted on the appointment or the dismissal of the personnel director and on all questions of welfare. They have extensive rights of co-decision, in particular with regard to the recruitment of workers and the fixing of wages, incentive payments, disciplinary rules, reduction of the workforce, as well as on all questions of principle concerning personnel management and industrial relations. Where the works council is opposed to a decision, the management may appeal to an arbitration body known as a committee of inquiry.

As regards organs of the works committee or joint consultation committee type which have been set up on a voluntary or contractual basis, there have been varying degrees of development in different countries.

In _Denmark_, where the agreement of 1964 concluded between the national trade union and employers' confederations applying to "joint consultation committees" attributed to these organs mainly information functions concerning production, the economic situation and working conditions of the undertaking, as well as consultation rights concerning the introduction of changes in production and measures for the benefit of the workers affected by the changes, the agreement which came into force in 1971 empowers these committees, now called "collaboration committees", to "take part in the decision making" relating to the principles governing working conditions and personnel policy. The parties are jointly responsible for applying the agreed principles, but the principles alone are thus subject to discussion and not the concrete decisions relating to these questions. The new Danish Basic Agreement of 1973, concluded by the same confederations, specifies in addition that "the right of the employer to direct and distribute work and to use appropriate manpower shall be exercised in conformity with the provisions of the collective agreements and in co-operation with the wage earners and their representatives, according to the agreements at any time existing between the Danish Federation of Trade Unions and the Danish Employers' Confederation".

In _Norway_, the production committees set up in undertakings, following a national agreement of 1945, have been replaced by joint organs of the works committee type. Subsequent agreements have progressively strengthened the powers of these organs, in particular by extending their rights of consultation. Thus, at the present time, all significant changes in production plans, methods, and plans for expansion, reduction or reorganisation, which affect the employees or their working conditions, must be discussed with these committees.

In _Sweden_, the agreement relating to works committees which was concluded in 1966 between the Swedish Employers' Confederation and the Swedish Confederation of Trade Unions is still in force, but a national agreement on rationalisation was concluded in June 1972, and new formulae have been adopted on a voluntary basis in a certain number of large and medium-sized undertakings (including a decentralisation of the representative organs in the form of department councils, contact or consultation groups, etc.). In the Götaverken shipyards, for example, a delegation which comprises four representatives of the employees (including foremen) and three representatives of management has been set up. This delegation establishes the principles governing recruitment, training and promotion policies of the undertaking. In addition it makes appointments to certain positions such as that of chief of personnel, works doctor and editor-in-chief of the works newspaper. It also acts in an advisory capacity with regard to the nomination of executives. Finally, it deals with disciplinary measures such as suspension.

In other Western European countries, on the contrary, the development has not been in the direction of such a strengthening of the activities of works councils or committees or consultative organs.

In _Italy_, the "internal committees" established in undertakings some twenty years ago by a national agreement, which only include a limited number of workers' representatives who deal mainly with individual grievances and welfare services, are tending at the present time to disappear, in certain large sectors of industry, in favour of trade union action, particularly by shop-floor delegates and their plant councils. Official recognition has, in fact, been given to trade union representation within the undertaking in France, by an Act of December, 1968, and in Italy, by an Act of May, 1970.

In the United Kingdom, the increasingly important role played by trade union delegates on the shop floor (shop stewards) and their committees has been accompanied by a decrease in number and a decline in importance of the joint consultation organs. However, these subsist, to some extent, particularly in undertakings where the trade unions are less strongly implanted. The British Industrial Relations Act of 1971 laid an obligation on the employer, under certain conditions, to provide information, mainly with a view to collective bargaining, and the subsequent Industrial Relations Code of Practice encourages the parties to set up consultation machinery even within negotiating bodies.

Outside Europe, except for the countries mentioned above, few important changes appear to have taken place during recent years. In India, the Joint Management Councils (JMC), which were set up from 1958 onwards through local agreements, according to a model agreement, after the relative failure of the joint works committees made compulsory under an Act of 1947, and which, in spite of their name, are mainly information and consultation bodies, often continue to meet with various difficulties (reluctance of employers and even of some trade unions, inter-trade union rivalries, tensions in industrial relations, illiteracy or semi-illiteracy of many workers, etc.). Some of these difficulties were mentioned by the National Committee on Labour in its 1969 report to the Central Government. It has sometimes been stated also that a more gradual introduction of such types of participation would be desirable, adapting them, if possible, to the technical and economic characteristics of the undertakings. In Japan, on the other hand, the joint councils, instituted in general by collective agreement, remain quite active in the private sector and even in the public sector, although perhaps to a lesser degree.

In a large number of French-speaking African countries, particularly in Dahomey, Gabon, Guinea, the Ivory Coast (where there exist some committees of plant delegates sometimes called trade union committees), Madagascar, Mali (in the private sector, while public undertakings have a system of participation in management), Morocco, Mauritania, Niger, Senegal, and Upper Volta, the personnel delegates elected by the workers or nominated by the trade unions - who are mainly responsible for dealing with grievances, supervising the application of legislation and collective agreements, notifying the labour inspectorate in case of need, and passing on their own suggestions or those of employees, sometimes also for administering welfare services - continue to provide the main means of participation within the undertaking. In the Republic of the Congo, the personnel delegates created under an Act of 1964, have, for several years, been replaced by the works trade union committee members. The above-mentioned personnel delegates who are found in French-speaking Africa are, to a large extent, comparable to the personnel delegates in France, who also deal mainly with grievances and carry out, in part, the functions of a works committee in cases where the workforce is smaller than that required by legislation for the creation of such a body. On the other hand, in many English-speaking African countries, shop stewards are found whose representative functions lead them to deal mainly with grievances but also, in a general way, with all problems of concern to the employees, including collective bargaining, and who, consequently, are somewhat similar to those who have existed for many years in, for example, Great Britain, Belgium and the Scandinavian countries.

In Latin America, in addition to the safety and health committees which are found in certain countries such as Mexico and Honduras, the trade union representatives in the undertaking in a number of countries not only continue to deal with the negotiation of collective agreements but also carry out various participation functions while supervising the application of these agreements, particularly in connection with the examination of grievances, or even participating in tripartite committees on dismissal or in other specialised committees. The same is true, to a certain extent, in several Asian countries such as Malaysia and Singapore.

4. Participation through trade
    union action

    (a) Trade union participation through
         collective bargaining in certain
         predominantly private enterprise
         economies

It is obviously only possible in a few pages to cover in a very general way the recent evolution of collective bargaining in industrialised[1] and developing countries, even when limiting this review to negotiations carried on at the level of the undertaking, which correspond more closely to our present subject. The most important aspect to be noted is that collective bargaining at the level of the undertaking, in so far as it is tending to broaden the scope of subject matter with which it deals and in this way to replace unilateral management decisions by decisions negotiated with the trade unions, is thus becoming an increasingly important means of participation. In many countries, in fact, collective bargaining is the only means of participation in decisions, or the most efficient means.

Among the industrialised countries where this type of participation in decisions within undertakings is most widespread mention may be made of Canada, the United States, Japan and the United Kingdom. In the United States, where the trade unions continue to oppose on principle the representation of workers in management organs, collective agreements, negotiated generally at the level of the undertaking, but also sometimes at the plant level, are the main form of participation. These negotiations have in fact reached a point over the years where they cover most decisions affecting employment and working conditions. The same is true in Canada and to a significant degree Japan. In the United Kingdom, the trade union delegates elected at the shop-floor level (shop stewards), of whom there were estimated to be some 300,000 in 1971,
----

[1] Cf. for further details concerning industrialised countries, International Labour Office, Collective bargaining in industrialised market economies, ILO, Geneva, 1974.

i.e. an average of one for every 50 or 60 unionised workers, whereas, at the same period, there were only some 3,000 full-time trade union officials, have for a certain number of years played an increasingly important role, while their committees enjoy a high degree of autonomy in collective bargaining. Some trade union leaders hold the view that everything occurring in the undertaking which workers wish to discuss should be subject to collective bargaining. Even in the other industrialised countries of Western Europe, where collective bargaining traditionally takes place at the industry level between the employers' organisations and trade unions, bargaining at the level of the undertaking has considerably developed in recent years as a result, in particular, of inflation.

Mention must also be made of the part played for some time by labour disputes, including "spontaneous" work stoppages, in promoting the extension of collective bargaining to the level of the undertaking in a number of European countries such as France, Italy, and the United Kingdom, and to a certain extent Belgium, the Federal Republic of Germany, the Netherlands and Sweden, among others. Many of these disputes have arisen from the desire to fix by agreement the wages which could actually be paid in the undertaking rather than merely having the minimum rates fixed at the industrial or national level. This, in many cases, has resulted in the phenomenon known as "wage drift". It has also happened that where full employment or even labour shortages exist, small groups of workers have become aware of their bargaining powers within undertakings which are made more vulnerable to such action by modern technology. In addition, a higher level of education has been observed among workers, particularly young workers, as well as an increased militancy along with a stronger desire to participate in decision-making.

Other factors which have contributed to the expansion of collective bargaining at the level of the undertaking include the desire to control actual working conditions in the undertaking and the general emphasis on demands of a qualitative nature, the rapid spread of information, through modern mass media, concerning improvements obtained or demanded elsewhere, etc. Technical change and "rationalisation" have, on the other hand, increased the importance of demands for job and income security and training, further training and retraining.

In most of the developing countries, collective bargaining took place until recently mainly at the level of the undertaking or plant, particularly in large undertakings. In general, in many countries in Africa, Latin America, the Caribbean, Asia and the Near and Middle East, the strengthening of the trade unions and the raising of the level of education of their leaders as well as of their members are contributing to a striking development of enterprise-level agreements. In a large number of developing countries, a trend is also evident - although to differing degrees - towards the conclusion of collective agreements which no longer cover wages alone but include a rapidly widening range of subjects. In a growing number of such countries, collective agreements are tending to become more and more lengthy texts, dealing with a great variety of matters of direct interest to the workers, who are thus becoming associated more and more with decisions which have to be taken in undertakings.

(b)   <u>Relations between management
       and the trade union in certain
       countries with a planned economy</u>

In the USSR and the other Eastern European countries, the
economic reform which was introduced towards the middle of the
sixties, and which resulted in increased autonomy for undertakings
through a more flexible system of decentralised planning and the
institution of undertaking funds built up by appropriations out of
profits when production targets fixed by the undertaking were
achieved or exceeded, was accompanied by an expansion of workers'
participation in the management of production and in numerous
decisions, in particular by the granting of increased powers to the
trade union committee of the undertaking or establishment.

This body had already, for many years, exercised important
functions, particularly as regards dismissals, welfare and safety
and health. The content of the collective agreements which are
concluded at the level of the undertaking between the trade union
committee and the management, in consultation with the workers, has
now been enlarged and these agreements are even more important
today. They deal, for example, with the fulfilment of state
economic plans and the application of scientific and technical
advances, the improvement of skills, of the organisation of work and
of productivity, as well as of the system of remuneration through
the development of material incentives in the form of bonuses and
allowances drawn from the corresponding undertaking fund. In
general, they define the mutual obligations of management, the trade
union committee and the personnel.

The regulations governing the rights of factory or
establishment trade union committees, adopted in 1971 in the USSR,
which replaced those of 1958, assign to these committees
responsibility for representing the interests of the employees in
all matters related to production and conditions of life and work as
well as for relations with the management and the local state
organs. The trade union committee must be consulted concerning the
appointment of management personnel. It has the right to take
decisions, after hearing the opinion of the management, on the use
to be made of the material incentives funds and also the funds for
socio-cultural needs (recreation and rest centres, sports,
libraries, etc.) and for the construction of housing for the
employees. The trade union committee of the undertaking, like that
of the workshop, takes part in the fixing of production standards
and the manning of work teams. Job classifications and wage rates
must also be established in agreement with this body.

Before raising a new matter with the management, the trade
union committee submits it for discussion by the workers' assembly.
The general assemblies of manual and clerical workers are, in fact,
one of the important means of participation by workers in the
management of production. In large undertakings, the assemblies
take the form of conferences attended by delegates elected by the
workers to represent them. In addition, the permanent production
committees play a particularly active role. These committees are
set up in all establishments employing at least 100 persons, and
their rights and obligations, which were previously fixed by a
regulation of 1958, were revised by a ruling adopted by the Council
of Ministers and the Central Council of Trade Unions in June 1973.
(In undertakings employing fewer than 100 workers, production

matters are considered by the general workers' assemblies.) These production committees are elected organs which include among their members both manual and clerical workers, representatives of the trade union committee of the undertaking or workshop, of the party organisations, of the technical and scientific associations and the association of inventors and experts in rationalisation. They deal with training and further training and examine all the matters relating to the improvement, organisation and planning of production as well as work discipline.

The trade union committee has wide powers of supervision and it can intervene with the competent organs to have the director and other managerial staff punished or even dismissed if they do not respect the terms of the collective agreement or the labour legislation or if they show bureaucratic tendencies or indifference to the workers' needs. In case of dispute between a worker and the management, the matter is usually submitted to a joint committee on labour disputes of the undertaking, while the trade union committee is empowered to take a final decision if the joint committee does not reach agreement.

A new element which is assuming a growing importance in Eastern Europe and particularly in the USSR is the practice of social planning, which has been spreading among the various undertakings since 1971. Long-term, detailed social development plans, which carry compulsory obligations, covering the important social measures to be taken at the level of the undertaking[1], are established jointly by the management and the trade union committee, after lengthy consulations.

These measures are concerned, among other matters, with the elimination of heavy work, the raising of the level of general and technical education of workers, the diminution of differential treatment between manual and non-manual workers and the increase of workers' participation in the management of production. This social planning, which is becoming an integral part of the planning of the undertaking and is related to the economic and production objectives set for it under the five-year state plan, lays down guidelines for future collective agreements in the undertaking.

With the exception of Yugoslavia, where the system in force has been described above, and to a certain extent Poland, the above-mentioned characteristics are found, with only some slight variations, in all the countries of Eastern Europe.

In Poland, at the same time as efforts were being made to decentralise the organisation of the public sector of the economy, workers' councils appeared spontaneously in a large number of industrial undertakings in 1956 and were given legal sanction by a law adopted in November of that year. The system of workers' management of undertakings, governed thereafter by an Act of 20 December 1958, has been revitalised since the end of 1970. The discussions at the Seventh Congress of Trade Unions, in November 1972, and numerous publications which have appeared in the country, are evidence of the growing interest which the system now arouses. It has been extended to other economic sectors such as commerce and

----

[1] The short-term measures are included in the collective agreement for the undertaking.

transportation, in addition to industry, construction and state farms where it had been applied originally. The principal organs are the following: the self-management conference, which meets every two or three months; the workers' council (which must include, apart from exceptional cases, at least a proportion of two-thirds of manual workers) and its praesidium; the shop or department workers' councils, which have developed relatively recently, and various specialised committees. The Party committee and the trade union committee are represented in each of these organs and play an active role therein.

In Hungary, where the trade union has the right to approve the appointment of heads of undertakings by the supervisory state body, the trade union committee in the undertaking in fact fulfils the functions of the general assembly of the personnel, but its policies are decided upon only after an exchange of views and discussions with the workers, in particular through production meetings and trade union meetings; this enables the committee to take into account the workers' proposals and criticisms. However, in the workshops and small plants, the assembly of the trade union members is the main form of participation.

In Romania, under the Labour Code of 1972, the general workers' assemblies constitute the supreme body for the collective management of undertakings and state and economic organisations. These assemblies elect the workers' representatives on the management board of each establishment who, along with the chairman of the trade union committee, the secretary of the Party organisation and the secretary of the Young Communist organisation in the undertaking, are members of the board as well as the management staff and specialists. These boards approve the five-year plan, the annual plan and the balance sheet. They decide on the employment or dismissal of certain management staff, and organise recruitment and training. They supervise the correct application of labour legislation and the provisions of collective agreements as well as of the system of remuneration, which henceforth includes a seniority bonus, and of safety and health standards, the carrying out of the production plan and the improvement of productivity and conditions of life and work. They report periodically to the general workers' assembly.

The German Democratic Republic, Bulgaria and Czechoslovakia operate a system very similar to that of the USSR. In the German Democratic Republic, an Act of November 1966, introduced important amendments and additions to the Labour Code, and detailed directives were issued in November 1971, concerning the annual conclusion of collective agreements. In Bulgaria, the importance attached to social planning has recently led to the extension to three years of the duration of collective agreements, while a five-year duration is under consideration, as is also the case in the USSR.

It may be that the recent tendency towards the concentration of industrial undertakings in the countries of Eastern Europe will give rise to problems of adjustment of the present participation structures. For example, already in Hungary, trade union councils have been created in the large merged undertakings, while the Romanian undertakings which have been joined together under the name of "industrial combines" are provided with a board of management in which a representative of the trade unions of the merged undertakings is included along with the managers of the combine and

of the said undertakings, as well as from three to ten of their
specialists. These combines also have general assemblies which play
a role comparable to that of the workers' assemblies of
undertakings; they comprise members of their board of management and
of the board of management of the merged undertakings, as well as
representatives of the personnel of the combine. In the USSR, a new
industrial structure was introduced in 1973. Since then,
undertakings, particularly small undertakings, are being merged in
large groupings in order to increase the efficiency of management.
This movement, which will continue up to 1975, may result in some
changes in the framework of industrial relations at the level of the
undertaking.

II. ARRANGEMENTS FOR ASSOCIATING WORKERS WITH THE DETERMINATION OF WORK ORGANISATION AT THE SHOP-FLOOR LEVEL

1. New concepts of work organisation

The systems described above are those in which workers
participate in decisions within undertakings through
representatives. While conceptually, of course, under these
systems, workers as a collectivity as well as individually are the
direct or indirect beneficiaries of, and participants in, the
decision-making process, such workers' participation schemes through
collective bargaining, consultation or workers' representation on
management bodies do not by themselves normally affect directly the
participation of workers in the organisation of work at the shop-
floor level. Decisions concerning the choice of equipment, method
of work, manning and job design generally remain within the realm of
management prerogatives. Although some input of workers' ideas and
experience may go into management decisions on these matters through
the use of suggestion schemes, or by informal, direct consultation
of workers and their shop-floor representatives by supervisors, at
various levels, as to the best way of doing a job, in general,
hierarchical structures of authority in enterprises have effectively
precluded the direct involvement of shop-floor workers in decisions
affecting the organisation of work, even where formalised
consultation or participation of workers takes place at higher
levels.

This absence of direct participation in decisions of immediate
concern to them in their daily work is held to be one of the major
ingredients of the dissatisfaction which is being increasingly
manifested in various ways among industrial and other types of
workers. With increasing exposure to a consumptionist society and
rising educational levels, workers' aspirations also rise for a more
satisfying work experience, including more control over the
organisation of their work, better knowledge of its end results,
greater freedom of movement, more chance for self-development and
promotion, wider scope for the exercise of initiative and the use of
their intellectual capacity and acquired skills. Younger workers,
in particular, are impatient with the limited scope of many jobs in
factory and office, the monotony of assembly-line types of activity
and the constraints of authoritarian methods of supervision. The
high rate of absenteeism and labour turnover, a general decline of
interest in work and increase of indifference and apathy leading to

carelessness and a lowering of standards of quality, which are common phenomena today in enterprises throughout the world, are widely attributed to the hiatus between the aspirations of workers and the realities of jobs as they are organised in many cases, and to the increasingly felt cleavage between workplace and life outside the factory or office.

These phenomena and methods to respond to these newly felt challenges have given rise to a series of experiments and efforts aimed at improving work organisation. Concepts such as "humanisation of work" or "better quality of working life" illustrate the growing concern over, and growing interest in, work organisation at the shop-floor level and increasing participation of workers in decisions concerning the manner in which their jobs are performed. This part of the Background Paper does not attempt to make an in-depth study of the present stage of thinking or of the results of the various experiments. Its sole purpose is to present the problem as background information for the benefit of the participants in the Oslo Symposium, to facilitate their discussions.

For decades, social scientists and other observers have denounced the excessive fragmentation and simplification of machine-paced tasks which characterise the scientific organisation of work popularised by Taylor[1], pointing out the meaningless nature of such jobs to workers and the sense of powerlessness they engender.[2] A few experiments - in particular those carried out by Hyacinthe Dubreuil in the Bat'a shoe company in the thirties[3] - demonstrated that workers organised in co-operative groups could take an active part in a wide range of decisions directly concerning their jobs without disrupting the flow of production, and, indeed, with salutary results on productivity and on worker attitudes within the plant. Such views have gradually gained a wider currency, under the influence of developments in management theory in recent years which stressed the effectiveness of a less authoritarian and more "participative" management style, and studies of worker motivation. Trade union pressures for better conditions in the workplace and a more human organisation of industrial work, and, in some countries, government interest in promoting systems of workers' participation in decisions, have also contributed to a widespread reconsideration of accepted forms of work organisation. The flattening out of the structure of authority in undertakings by the delegation of decision-making power to the shop-floor level is thus beginning to appear as a complementary trend to the promotion of worker participation through representatives.

At the present time, a great deal of experimentation is taking place in an effort to adjust the social and technical systems of production to more livable patterns of work, allowing the workers a greater span of decision-making power on the shop-floor. However
----

[1] Cf. F.W. Taylor, Scientific management, New York, Harper, 1947 (first published in 1911).

[2] Cf. for example Georges Friedmann, Le travail en miettes, Paris, Gallimard, 1956.

[3] Cf. Hyacinthe Dubreuil, L'exemple de Bat'a, La Libération des initiatives individuelles dans une entreprise géante, Paris, Grasset, 1936.

modest may be the practical achievements so far, in terms of their
over-all impact on the workforce in the plant or the industry
concerned, some of these experiments do appear to represent a new
vision of the workplace for the future. But breaking as they do
into traditional patterns of management structure, work organisation
and labour-management relations, they often raise difficulties of
implementation and are nowhere accepted without question or
opposition.

Most of the known experiments in this field at present are
being carried out in the industrialised countries of Europe and
North America. Only a limited number of cases have been fully
reported and many of the changes have been introduced too recently
for the results to have been evaluated clearly. No two experiments
are identical, but in spite of this variety the basic concepts and
techniques used show certain similarities, the main differences
being due to the over-all objectives of the initiators and the
extent to which a fundamental change in the attribution of decision-
making power is actually sought.

Very often, the more direct association of workers with the
organisation of their work is being introduced within the context of
a broader movement towards the improvement of the whole working
environment and physical conditions of work, which involves changes
in many aspects of the workplace situation. Some of the following
types of innovations are found in many of the present experiments:

- Changes in the technology or the mechanics of the production
  process. For example, the reorganisation of assembly-line
  conveyor-belt systems so that work can be performed on a
  stationary object, the product can be moved at the will of the
  worker or automatically placed so as to facilitate work in a
  more natural and less tiring position; the shortening of
  assembly lines and their arrangement so that the product is
  visible at all times to the operators; the introduction of
  automatic devices to handle repetitive or dangerous
  operations.

- Changes in the physical environment of the workplace. For
  example, improvements in plant layout allowing for more
  spacious and better lighted work areas, better ventilation and
  noise control and general plant housekeeping; grouping of
  operations in order to create a more intimate atmosphere; more
  efficient arrangements for the supply of material and parts,
  by the constitution of "buffer stocks" which allow workers
  greater flexibility in the pace of work.

- Changes in the design of jobs. For example, the enlargement
  of the scope of operators' jobs to include some preparatory
  and maintenance operations as well as quality control; the
  rotation of workers between different operations on assembly
  lines or in continuous-flow processes; the lengthening of the
  work cycle in production, sometimes to the extent that one
  worker can complete a whole series of operations or even build
  an entire unit; rotation of workers between preassembly
  operations and work on the assembly line.

- Organisation of work in autonomous groups. For example, the
  setting up of production groups, the size of which may range
  from three to forty workers in different circumstances, with

responsibility for one production assignment which constitutes a homogeneous unit; such groups usually have varying degrees of freedom to organise the work and the interchange of jobs among workers within the group, to plan breaks and to take or propose other decisions concerning the work within the limits of an assigned production goal or schedule.

- Changes in the conditions of work. For example, new systems of wage calculation and payment, including group incentives, to take account of changing job structures; more flexible time schedules and individualised pace of work.

- Changes in the methods and contents of training, to broaden the range of skills of workers, increase the flexibility of the workforce and improve use of human resources.

Many of the above types of changes, which are designed to combat the monotony and fatigue of repetitive jobs, result in an enlargement of workers' power of decision-making at the level of the execution of work, for example, in the arrangement of job rotation and break schedules within a work group, increased authority to call for supplies, to reject defective products, to make needed repairs and even sometimes in personnel matters such as the replacement of absent workers or the selection of new members of the group. In a few instances, the authority of the group has been extended to the planning of production schedules over a certain period of time, even as long as three months in advance. Many decisions formerly taken by supervisors concerning job assignments and work methods now form part of the operators' daily responsibilities. Relations with supervisors are thus altered; the latter assume functions of a more technical, advisory nature, providing assistance in the solution of shop-floor problems and generally acting in a supportive rather than a managerial role. First line supervisors may even be dispensed with almost entirely, being replaced by a team leader chosen by the members of the work group in a number of experiments. Similarly, the inspection staff may be released for more conceptual tasks, such as the development of standards, where routine decisions regarding quality control are largely delegated to the operators themselves.

Workers may also participate at the preparatory stage in the planning and implementation of changes in work organisation. A notable characteristic of some of the experiments undertaken has been the direct involvement of shop-floor workers, along with members of management and technical specialists, in the analysis of problems related to production systems, suggestions for improvements in methods of work or workplace conditions and the development of new job designs, plans for layout of new plants and even changes in the technology and methods of production. Special joint committees or working groups have been set up for this purpose, at various levels, in some plants considering the introduction of innovations, to provide an opportunity for operators to express their views and to enable production engineers, designers, work study personnel and other managerial staff to draw on the operators' ideas and practical experience. Such groups have only advisory powers, but in practice they have exercised a definite influence in many cases on the final management decisions or on the solutions later reached by negotiated agreement. Joint consultative structures set up on an ad hoc basis to help initiate changes have often continued in existence after the planning period, meeting regularly to settle problems arising during the running-in period or to plan the subsequent introduction of further changes.

- 24 -

Another feature of this trend in some countries is the participation of workers in the introduction of such changes through their representatives at the plant level or through established collective bargaining procedures. Parallel with the development of direct consultation between management and workers on these questions, workplace conditions and work organisation are increasingly becoming the object of trade union demands in collective negotiations at plant, regional, industrial and national levels, in accordance with the industrial relations system and bargaining structure. In some of the socialist countries, trade unions have taken the initiative in many instances in promoting workplace innovation.

2. Promotion of worker participation
   in the organisation of work:
   Different approaches and motivating
   factors

The association of the workers concerned in decisions relating to their job may be seen as instrumental - as a means of creating a sense of personal involvement of workers in the aims of the undertaking, of making work more meaningful, of increasing individual satisfaction in work by enhancing responsibility and interest in the job; as a means of improving employees' performance, of achieving higher levels of productivity; as a means of facilitating acceptance of change in the production technology, work methods or structure of the organisation; or as a means of forestalling potential grievances and employee-management conflict. Participation at this level may, on the other hand, be considered as an end in itself - a system which embodies respect for human values and the dignity of the individual or as a just sharing of power in the enterprise in recognition of the workers' essential contribution to its functioning. Such underlying preoccupations inevitably condition the type of experiments undertaken and the way in which changes are introduced; but in many cases there is a complex interweaving of different influences, motivations and approaches which are giving shape to the present trends in work reorganisation.

Management approaches have been widely influenced by the research carried out by behavioural scientists, for example, the analyses of R. Likert[1] and Douglas McGregor[2], which stressed the importance of making fuller use of the latent potential of workers through management methods based on the assumption that the average worker is willing to accept responsibility and will respond to the opportunity of using his intellectual faculties in larger measure. In Likert's studies, high morale and high performance were shown to be associated with the development of work groups where the leader and subordinates worked together on solving problems, management playing only a supportive role. Systems of management where all members of the organisation were able to influence decisions thus reached higher levels of efficiency.

----

[1] Cf. R. Likert, New patterns and management, New York, McGraw-Hill, 1961.

[2] Cf. D. McGregor, The human side of enterprise, New York, McGraw-Hill, 1960, and Leadership and motivation, Cambridge, Mass., M.I.T., 1966.

Another current of research, represented by A.H. Maslow[1] and Frederick Herzberg[2], concentrated on the study of worker motivation and the design of jobs which would afford workers an opportunity of satisfying their higher needs beyond the basic material requirements of income, shelter and security. These authors concluded that management efforts directed solely towards the improvement of physical conditions and human relations in the enterprise could do little to create positive satisfaction and commitment among workers, whereas the enrichment of tasks and the introduction of a more flexible organisation of work to give greater scope for initiative and self-fulfilment could be vastly more rewarding.

These theories have been tested in practice by a number of experiments in "job enrichment" undertaken at management's initiative, often with the assistance of social science researchers in analysing work content and designing new job structures. Among the earliest and most comprehensive applications were carried out by the American Telephone and Telegraph Company in the United States[3], which, after more than a decade of experimentation, continues to pursue this approach to work organisation in many different services throughout its vast organisation. In this case, as in other similar experiments, management was motivated by problems of a technical, economic or social nature for which job enrichment techniques appeared to provide a solution - for example, recruitment difficulties, excessively high labour turnover and absenteeism rates, over-manning or frequency of employee grievances and customer complaints. The introduction of a more "participative" management style and the improvement of job design are reported in several cases to have given good results in terms of worker attitudes and productivity.

Taken even in its most limited sense, the job enrichment approach provides greater scope for workers' participation in day-to-day decisions immediately affecting their work. It tends to introduce more flexible methods of control, less direct supervision, increased communication between workers and supervisors and an improved flow of information to employees at the shop-floor level, including data relevant to the execution of their jobs (production charts and schedules) and information concerning their own performance. Job enrichment techniques, such as the rotation of tasks, the broadening of qualifications and responsibilities of workers, and the enhancement of the intrinsic interest of the job, form an essential element of many more broadly-conceived experiments in work reorganisation. The fact remains nonetheless that the introduction of such changes alone often represents a change in management style rather than a modification of the structure of authority in the enterprise. Employee participation in preparing the introduction of changes in work organisation has in some
----

[1] Cf. A.H. Maslow, Motivation and personality (2nd edition), New York, Harper and Row, 1970.

[2] Cf. F. Herzberg, B. Mausner and B.B. Snyderman, Motivation to work, New York, Wiley, 1959 and F. Herzberg, Work and the nature of man, Cleveland and New York, the World Publishing Company, 1966.

[3] These experiments are fully described by Robert N. Ford, in Motivation through the work itself, New York, American Management Association Inc. 1969.

instances simply taken the form of answering questionnaires designed to locate the sources of dissatisfaction and to suggest possible avenues of improvement. Advance information or consultation of workers concerned is, in fact, expressly discouraged by the job enrichment theorists from the fear that this might confuse the issues at stake and raise false expectations.[1] It is also thought by some that giving employees a sense of participation will not produce any lasting benefits; moreover, such procedures are felt to conflict with management's rights and to be ineffective and disruptive in practice.[2] The hierarchical structure thus remains intact, the level of decision-making accessible to workers being limited to matters immediately related to their tasks.

Much more profound changes in the distribution of decision-making power are envisaged by the socio-technical systems theory, an approach developed several decades ago by a group of researchers of the Tavistock Institute of Human Relations in the United Kingdom.[3] Their studies stemmed from the notion of the "joint optimisation" of the social and technical systems within an enterprise, - i.e. the technology of production and the organisation of work - each being designed in relation to the other to serve the best interests of worker satisfaction and technical efficiency. Great emphasis was laid on the value of workers' sharing responsibility for decisions concerning their jobs through the organisation of work in groups or teams, in order to allow maximum scope for individual development, while, at the same time, the technical systems are adapted to the human needs of operators as well as to organisational requirements.

This approach necessitates a thorough functional analysis of the operation of the plant or undertaking concerned, since the optimum solution must be tailored to fit the needs of a particular organisation. The changes proposed may profoundly affect the structure of authority and are therefore developed in consultation with all levels and categories of personnel involved - engineers and designers, work study personnel, supervisors, foremen and shop-floor operatives as well as plant management - in order to draw on their experience in redesigning the work in the most effective and satisfactory manner and to obtain prior consent of those affected. This process, once launched, is irreversible; it would be virtually impossible to return to the former method of work after such a complete upheaval.

The difficulties of obtaining the co-operation of staff for such experiments, the time, effort and expense involved, the uncertainty as regards the results and apprehensions about embarking on a course which may lead further than is intended on the road to workers' participation in decisions, have undoubtedly acted as restraining factors, and the number of known practical applications

----

[1] Cf. Robert N. Ford, op. cit. pp. 121-124, and F. Herzberg, "One more time: how do you motivate employees?" in Harvard business review, January-February 1968, p. 61.

[2] Cf. for example, Thomas H. Fitzgerald, "Why motivation theory doesn't work", in Harvard business review, July-August 1971, pp. 42-43.

[3] Cf. for example, Dr. F.E. Emery, "The democratisation of the workplace", in Manpower and applied psychology, Vol. 1 No. 2.

of these theories remains small. Norway was the first country to pioneer in this field, a decade ago, by undertaking a series of experiments carried out with the advice and assistance of researchers from the Tavistock Institute, and within the framework of a programme to promote industrial democracy which was developed jointly by the central employers' and workers' organisations.[1] In one of the plants selected for the trials, engaged in the manufacture of electric radiators, the tasks of production, supervision, planning, maintenance and handling of goods, which were formerly fragmented and assigned to specialised workers, have been regrouped and entrusted to autonomous teams composed of from fifteen to forty workers. Each group elects annually its own leader, who is responsible for co-ordination with other groups and for contacts with management where necessary. The group leaders and the local plant management form a committee competent to take decisions on production planning, financial management and all aspects of the plant's development. Within the groups, workers decide among themselves the distribution of jobs and are trained to be interchangeable. The autonomy of the groups extends to the planning of production schedules - initially for a four weeks' period, but later, at the request of the groups, a planning period of three months was introduced. Another experiment of this type was carried out by the Norsk Hydro Company in a new plant in Porsgrunn, producing chemical fertilizer. Work in that plant has been organised in five teams of twelve workers each, each team being composed of three work groups of four workers each who are trained to carry out all the operations in one particular area of the work, including maintenance and cleaning of work areas as well as quality control. A special "action committee" composed of an outside researcher, the plant manager, representatives of the local union, of the supervisors and of the personnel department, met weekly to watch and guide the experiment in the early stages; later this work was taken over by the "department committees" which had been set up throughout Norwegian industry under an agreement concluded between the central unions and employers' organisations in 1967.[2]

National-level agreements between employers' and workers' organisations have set the background for experiments in the reorganisation of work at the plant level in Sweden and Denmark, as well as in Norway. The trade unions in these countries have therefore been involved at both levels in the discussion and planning of changes on the shop floor. Since the thrust of this movement was to promote a more democratic form of organisation at the workplace, great emphasis has been placed in these experiments not only on the enlargement of workers' participation in day-to-day decisions concerning the organisation of work, but also in their involvement at the planning stage when new systems are being
----

[1] The first phase of this programme was reported on by F.E. Emery, Einar Thorsrud and Eric Trist in Form and content in industrial democracy, London, Tavistock, 1969, first published in Norwegian in "Industrielt Demokrati", Oslo University Press, 1964.

[2] These Norwegian experiments have been described by Yves Delamotte in "Recherches en vue d'une organisation plus humaine du travail industriel", La documentation française, Paris 1972: the Norsk Hydro experiment was related by Nancy Foy, "Industrial democracy at Norsk Hydro", in European business, Winter 1973, pp. 30-36.

introduced. In both Norway and Sweden, joint research bodies have
been set up on the central level to study methods of job redesign,
job enrichment, rotation of jobs and the organisation of semi-
autonomous work groups, and to assist plants in the introduction of
such changes.

In Sweden, a parallel impulse for such experiments has come
from the national employers' organisation, which has been active in
stimulating the search for new work systems among its members with
a view to promoting job satisfaction and higher productivity. It is
noteworthy that the motivating factors mentioned above - the need to
rationalise production in a competitive market, difficulties of
recruitment and higher labour turnover, absenteeism and other
symptoms of worker alienation - are urgent problems in these
countries as elsewhere, impelling managements to seek solutions in
a reorganisation of the workplace. The theories and techniques of
job enrichment and the restructuring of work in autonomous groups
have had a wide influence. But the particular labour relations
system in these countries, characterised by a long tradition of
joint co-operation at the national level, has provided a framework
for a co-operative approach to innovations at the workplace level.
Thus, even where the initiative for changes has come from the
management, the trade unions as well as the workers themselves have
been directly involved, and the systems developed have sought to
introduce a very large degree of worker autonomy in the execution of
work and participation in the planning process.

In the SAAB and Volvo automobile companies, for example, a
policy has been followed for a number of years of encouraging plant
managements to develop ways of putting into effect certain
principles of worker participation in the organisation of work.
This has resulted in a variety of innovations; for example, in the
SAAB-Scania works in Södertalje, producing truck chassis and
engines, the management worked closely with representatives of all
the unions as well as technical specialists in a "reference group"
set up to define objectives for experiments and to select areas for
trials; work groups, including operators, were then established in
the selected areas to make suggestions for changes in present
systems of work; eventually, the assembly work was organised in
production groups composed of operators representing the various
trades involved. These groups were given complete responsibility
for organising and carrying out an entire operation, under the
general supervision of development groups responsible for preparing
production plans and objectives. Another experiment carried out in
a plant producing SAAB 99 engines involved the redesign of the
assembly line to allow workers to build an entire engine at their
own pace, within an over-all production goal; this design was
developed by a project group which drew on the experience of
operators, supervisors and other personnel.[1] Many plants in the
Volvo company have also introduced systems of group production which
involve the rotation of workers between a number of different work
stations on the assembly line or the formation of a small team of
workers responsible for one work assignment which they organise
independently. Such changes have in every case been planned in
consultation with union representatives as well as the operators
----

[1] Cf. Jan-Peder Norstedt and Stefan Agureū, The Saab-Scania
Report, Swedish Employers' Confederation, Technical Department,
1973.

concerned. At present, two new plants are being built on designs worked out by project groups in which unions and operating personnel take part, and which incorporate many of the new concepts and techniques developed during previous experiments to provide for group work and greater worker autonomy.[1]

In other countries, a great many different types of experiments designed to allow for greater participation of workers in decisions concerning the organisation of work have been carried out, mainly at the initiative of management. Trade union pressures have, however, played a determining role in some instances. While the unions are rarely involved directly in consultations with management concerning the restructuring of work or the redesign of jobs (the absence of plant-level union representation hinders such consultation in some instances) they frequently exercise an influence on these changes through the medium of collective bargaining. Some trade unions are suspicious of new forms of shop-floor organisation which they believe are designed to obtain higher productivity at the workers' expense, or to eliminate jobs, and they also may fear that worker participation at this level could encourage the "integration" of employee and management interests and a decline of support for the collective aims of the workforce. Thus, in general, unions have sought to respond to the undercurrent of workers' dissatisfaction with work and working conditions and their demand for greater autonomy in their jobs by an adaptation of collective bargaining to new demands.

An increasing number of non-economic issues are being raised in negotiations between trade unions and employers in a number of countries, relating specifically to the organisation of work (speed of assembly lines, overtime hours, workloads, etc.) and some agreements have been concluded which provide for an enlargement of the work cycle, rotation of jobs, or opportunities for promotion and improved qualifications of unskilled and semi-skilled workers, through a reorganisation of work. In Italy, for example, in the Olivetti company producing mechanical and electronic equipment, which has made extensive experiments in autonomous group work among assembly line operators, using job enrichment principles, the unions have negotiated a series of agreements providing, in particular, for the promotion of a specified number of operators to more highly skilled jobs over a certain period within the framework of these changes.[2] The national agreements negotiated in 1973 in the Italian metal trades contain provisions designed to foster occupational mobility of workers through training and redesign of jobs to provide for interchangeability; several complementary enterprise level agreements provide for advance information of plant-level trade union representatives concerning the introduction of new methods of work and joint study of the effects of such changes. Unions in the automobile industry in the Federal Republic of Germany have also
----

[1] Cf. Press Information published by AB Volvo Head Office, Communication and Public Affairs, Göteborg, Sweden.

[2] The Olivetti experiments are described by Yves Delamotte, op. cit.; Frederico Butera, "Experiences of advances in work organisation: Olivetti", paper prepared for OECD International Seminar on Advances in Work Organisation, 3-6 April 1973, Paris, and Francesco Novara, "Job enrichment in the Olivetti Company", International Labour Review, Vol. 108, No. 4, October 1973, p. 283.

bargained for an improvement of jobs and elimination of monotony on assembly lines and in continuous processes; an agreement concluded in October 1973 between the metalworkers' union, I.G. Metall, and the employers' organisation representing companies in Nord Wurtemburg-Baden included provision for a minimum length of the work cycle (one minute and a half) and increased rest periods. In the publicly owned Renault automobile company in France, which has introduced a variety of new systems of organising assembly work, on an experimental basis, with a view to the enlargement of tasks, the plant-level agreement signed in January 1973 contains a provision whereby the management undertakes to put into practice the positive conclusions of these experiments, although the latter were initiated by management without prior consultation or information of the unions concerned.

Collective bargaining has provided an avenue for the introduction of changes in work organisation in the United Kingdom where such innovations have frequently taken place within the framework of productivity agreements which opened the way for a rationalisation of operations and the modification of works rules. One such case is the nylon-spinning factory of the ICI at Gloucester, where a productivity agreement signed by the company made it possible for management to work out, in co-operation with the unions at the plant level, a more flexible system of operations giving the workers greater freedom of movement and autonomy in the organisation of their work and production schedules. Shop stewards and workers were closely associated from the start in the planning of the changes, through shop-floor discussion groups, which worked out job descriptions and discussed new patterns of work, including proposals to allow semi-skilled workers to perform operations falling within the purview of craft unions. These proposals were then negotiated by the company with a joint committee of shop stewards representing the various unions concerned. This system continues to function; the bargaining process intervenes after the problems arising in the course of the work have been discussed and solutions outlined jointly with those directly concerned in the shop-floor discussion groups.[1]

Although plant-level bargaining is customary in the United States and Canada, trade unions have rarely participated in experiments in work reorganisation, many of which have been of the job enrichment type, often carried out in non-unionised undertakings. In one case, the Aluminium Company of Canada obtained the co-operation of the union in carrying out an experiment in more flexible work systems in a foundry operation, which involved a need for renegotiation of some of the terms of the collective agreement related to seniority rights and job evaluation.[2] The unions in these countries have on the whole continued to focus their main attention

----

[1] For description and discussion of this and other United Kingdom experiments, see: Stephen Cotgrove, Jack Dunham, Clive Vamplew, The nylon spinners, London, George Allen and Unwin, 1971; W.W. Daniel and Neil McIntosh, The right to manage, London, Political and Economic Planning (P.E.P.), 1972; W.W. Daniel, Beyond the wage-work bargain, P.E.P. Broadsheet 519, July 1970; R.O. Clarke, D.J. Fatchett and B.C. Roberts, Workers' participation in management in Britain, London, Heinemann Educational Books, 1972.

[2] Cf. International Conference on the Quality of Working Life, 24-29 September 1972, Arden House, Harriman, New York, communication of Mrs. Judith T. Acher, Department of Human Relations, Waterloo University, Ontario, Canada.

on the traditional bargaining issues such as remuneration, hours of work, and job security, but some interest is beginning to be voiced at the level of the national and international confederations in the "democratisation" of the workplace and the need for greater worker participation in the organisation of their tasks, better communications between workers and management and the elimination of arbitrary managerial authority in work decisions.[1] In this perspective, the 1973 agreements concluded in the automobile industry in the United States and Canada provided for the setting up, in each of the major companies, of a joint committee for the improvement of the quality of working life, with three members each from the union and the company, empowered to study and analyse possible changes in the organisation of work and to undertake experiments.

In some of the socialist countries, the problems of worker dissatisfaction appear also to occur in terms of high turnover rates and absenteeism, especially among younger workers. Considerable interest has been shown in studies of worker motivation and methods of promoting worker participation in decisions at the shop-floor level and better opportunities for self-fulfilment, as an antidote to these trends.[2] A great deal of psycho-social research is being carried out concerning the organisation of work with a view to improving both physical and psychological conditions on assembly lines - for example, in the "Red Dawn" knitting mill in the USSR, a careful analysis of operations has resulted in the arrangement of work in some operations so that it is no longer paced by the moving line and workers enjoy more freedom and variety in their daily activity. At the Volga automobile plant in Togliattigrad, built with the assistance of Fiat, assembly workers have been organised in "brigades" of 15 to 25 workers who carry out a sequence of up to 20 operations; the operators are trained to do a number of different operations and jobs are rotated among the members of the group. These arrangements are laid down in the collective agreement for the undertaking, which specifies that the administration agrees to

----

[1] Cf. for example, statements adopted by the International Metalworkers' Federation at its Twenty-second Congress in Lausanne, October 1971, on "democratisation at the workplace"; by the Executive Council of the Canadian Labour Congress, in December 1972; by the International Union, United Automobile, Aerospace and Agricultural Implement Workers of America, in Proceedings, UAW Special Convention, 22-23 March 1973, p. 53.

[2] F. Herzberg reports in Work and the nature of man, pp. 120-121, that he was invited to assist in a survey carried out among engineers in a locomotive works in Budapest, Hungary, concerning motivation of workers. Similar studies have been undertaken by Soviet researchers at the University of Leningrad, reported in Man and his work, edited by A.G. Zdravomyslov, V.P. Rozhin and V.A. Iadov, published in English by International Arts and Sciences Press, Inc., White Plains, New York, 1970 (first published in Moscow in 1967). The Czechoslovak Institute for Labour Research in Bratislava has carried out a number of studies on job satisfaction, reported in its review Syntéza.

create conditions allowing members of brigades to learn related
trades so as to avoid monotony in assembly line operations.[1]

Workers' participation in shop-level decisions in this country
is mainly exercised through the trade unions, which are active at
all levels in Soviet enterprises in the organisation of production
along the most efficient lines as well as in the improvement of
conditions of work, safety and welfare of workers. In the Volga
plant, for example, the union has co-operated in the setting up of
a laboratory for psycho-physiological studies, in order to analyse
operations and design the most satisfactory work methods, taking
account of workers' needs and aspirations. Great emphasis is also
placed on the improvement of qualifications of the workforce and the
provision of training to facilitate their promotion and
interchangeability. There is thus evidence in socialist countries
of a strong trend towards greater worker autonomy on the job.
However, decisions in matters relating to the organisation of work
still appear to be taken through the established procedures.

3. General observations and questions

The above trends and experiments have so far affected only a
very small number of workers in relation to the total labour force
in the countries concerned. Full evaluation of the results is not
yet available in most cases. But some preliminary observations may
be made, on the basis of reported experience, regarding both the
postive aspects and the problems and questions raised.

Job satisfaction

In terms of worker satisfaction, the innovations providing
greater scope for initiative and real power of decision concerning
the organisation of work have, in many cases, elicited a positive
response. It is felt that workers on the whole seem to enjoy the
increased autonomy on the job and the experience of having their
views taken into consideration by management in the planning of work
organisation has overcome initial scepticism in many instances.
There are, however, certain elements in the workforce who are
opposed to changes which disrupt the routine of repetitive jobs and
require more mental agility; others have complained of increased
fatigue due to the increased complexity of their tasks or a heavier
workload. However, job satisfaction is not only determined by the
influence workers may have on the organisation of their work. It
greatly depends also on their remuneration and general working
conditions which are normally the outcome of collective bargaining
between employers and trade unions.

Productivity

Job satisfaction is an unstable component of the work
situation, difficult to measure. A decline in absenteeism and
labour turnover occurring after the introduction of a system of
worker participation in decisions at shop-floor level may be due to
----

[1] Viaggio a Togliattigrad, Resoconto di una delegazione di
studio CGIL, Roma, Editrice Sindacale Italiana, 1971.

changes in general conditions on the employment market as much as to
the increased commitment of workers to their jobs as a result of the
experiments.   But these factors have given measurable benefits to
certain undertakings where experiments have taken place, at least
where an appreciable number of workers were involved. Productivity
increases and improvements in the standards of quality of products
and services have, in most cases, been reported and even been one of
the essential motivating factors for introducing such experiments.
Since the reorganisation of work has frequently taken place in the
context of a rationalisation of operations, or under pressure of
high market competition, economies were, in such cases, envisaged
from the start.   But even where the innovations were introduced in
connection with the construction of new plants involving large
investments, a reduction of the number of workers required for a
given level of production has often been a feature of these
projects.   Some anxiety has therefore been expressed, especially by
trade union spokesmen, with regard to the long-term effect on job
opportunities should such systems be widely applied.

Effects on the workforce and the employment market

     The applicability of certain forms of more participative
systems of work organisation to different types of production
processes and service operations and to different categories of
personnel seems to have been demonstrated by the diverse experiments
which have been carried out in the countries mentioned above.
However, not all workers appear to be equally adaptable to such
changes. The difficulties of older workers, handicapped workers, or
those who lack basic education, in learning a variety of operations
or adjusting to an extended work cycle have been noted. Some firms
have made a careful selection of employees to take part in the
development and implementation of new work systems or have called
for volunteers; in most cases the changes have been introduced
cautiously with allowance for a considerable period of training and
adaptation of those concerned.   There have, however, been some
experiments which involved the entire personnel of a department or
plant where solutions have been worked out to provide a range of
choices of jobs suitable to the varying capacity of workers to
participate fully in the new types of organisation.   Some
apprehensions have been expressed regarding the possibility that the
employment market might eventually be sharply split, with, on the
one hand, the jobs allowing for a wider participation in decision-
making reserved for those better able to adapt to them and the
general run of monotonous, low-skilled jobs being left to the weaker
and less qualified members of the workforce.   Special training
measures may be necessary to enable all types of workers, including
foreign labour, to take advantage of new opportunities becoming
available.

Learning to work as a group

     The organisation of work in autonomous production groups often
places considerable strain on both workers and supervisors. To
handle discussions of work problems and find solutions on a co-
operative basis requires skills and a talent for leadership quite
different from that required by the usual authoritative supervisory
role.   Workers on fixed, repetitive assignments are unaccustomed to

sharing in decisions in a spirit of mutual understanding.
Conflictual situations are bound to arise, caused by personality
clashes, differences over job distribution and rotation or even the
refusal of workers of different nationalities or ethnic groups to
work together as a team. There is also the danger that production
groups will work in competitition with one another and will try to
exclude from their midst less capable or weaker members. By and
large, however, the experience seems to show that a co-operative
organisation of work in teams has had favourable results, not only
in economic terms, through the greater flexibility of a system where
workers are interchangeable within a group responsible for one unit
of production, but also in terms of the satisfaction workers derive
from the social interchange, the greater variety in their work and
the broader scope of responsibility in organising the production
effort.

Relation to systems of workers' participation through representatives

The relationship of systems of worker participation in plant-
level decisions through representatives to the expansion of
participation on the shop-floor level is not clearly defined, and
is, in many respects, a controversial issue. While the worker has,
of course, human aspirations towards self-expression, sense of
purpose in his work and expanding his area of initiative and the
field in which he can co-decide on the way his job is to be
performed, he also has essential requirements in terms of
remuneration, protection against occupational hazards, job security,
reasonable hours, holidays with pay and other working conditions.
History and experience have demonstrated that, in order to have
these requirements fulfilled, he must act as a member of a
collectivity, through his trade union. The various methods of
workers' participation through representatives, be it collective
bargaining, or the action of a works council, or the role played by
a workers' representative on a management or supervisory board, may
therefore be seen as a wider framework within which experiments with
workers' participation in work organisation at the shop-floor level
may be tried out. There have been cases of experiments with shop-
floor participation in which trade unions or other types of workers'
representatives have been by-passed or have not been associated.
However, it is hardly thinkable that efforts at "humanising" work
relationships by giving workers a greater say in the organisation of
their work could be successful on a larger scale unless they have
the full support of the trade unions.

Government intervention

Experiments taking place at the enterprise level have
attracted the interest of governments in several of the
industrialised countries with market economies. Some experiments
have been carried out in state-owned enterprises and government
administrations. Although the State in these countries does not
normally intervene in the organisation of work within private
undertakings, government agencies in Canada, France, the United
Kingdom and the United States have made special studies of the new
methods of work being introduced and attempted to evaluate their
significance. In some of these countries, action has been taken
with a view to encouraging joint consideration by employers and

workers of these trends - for example, by the setting up of a tripartite committee, as in the United Kingdom, or by the establishment of a special government agency empowered to advise the parties and to carry out research, as in France. A more direct approach, through the financing of joint analyses of problems at the plant level, with expert assistance from outside, at the request of the parties, has been attempted by the National Productivity Commission in the United States. Other initiatives, such as special research on the causes of absenteeism and the development of techniques for measuring worker satisfaction, are being pursued in these countries with a view to adapting labour and social policies to workers' real needs and aspirations.

Applicability to developing countries

As shown in the first part of this report, most developing countries in Africa, Latin America and Asia and the Near and Middle East have introduced some form of worker participation in decisions at the enterprise level. In some developing countries people are wondering whether it would be appropriate, in the context of a developing economy, to introduce participative systems in the organisation of work such as have been described above. There is obviously no straight forward answer to this question and the differences between developing countries are so great that they preclude any simplistic approach. What can be said by way of a general comment is that, in a situation of unemployment and underemployment, widespread poverty and a very limited degree of industrialisation, there would not seem to be as much incentive for management as in the highly industrialised countries to experiment with workers' participation in work organisation at the shop-floor level, while trade unions must give their priority consideration to obtaining or ensuring fair pay and acceptable working conditions for their members. However, in some developing countries conditions are changing rapidly.

III.   FINAL REMARKS

The brief survey given in this Background Paper shows two things: first, that the drive for workers' participation in decisions within undertakings is a worldwide phenomenon which, as a basic proposition, is no longer contested, the discussions being centred on the form of workers' participation; and second, that the formulae applied or sought throughout the world show an immense variety ranging from workers' self-management to collective bargaining, including works' councils or other bodies and workers' representation on managerial bodies, and extending to the workplace level where workers are associated with the determination of the manner in which their jobs are to be carried out.

It is not surprising, therefore, that this paper has deliberately refrained from attempting an international definition of the term or concept of "participation". This problem of terminology was considered by the ILO Technical Meeting on the Rights of Trade Union Representatives and Participation of Workers in Decisions within Undertakings, held in 1967, whose final report contains the following paragraphs concerning this important issue:

40. At the beginning of its deliberations on the second item on its agenda, the Meeting considered the question of whether it was possible to arrive at an internationally agreed definition of the term "participation", in order to elucidate what was meant by the expression "participation of workers in decisions within undertakings". It found that it was not possible to arrive at such a definition, as the term "participation" was interpreted differently by different categories of people in different countries and at different times. Several experts expressed the view that, taken in its widest possible sense, it might be so all-embracing that it tended to become almost meaningless.

41. The exchange of views which the experts had, and which confirmed the way in which the subject matter had been presented in the report prepared by the Office, showed, however, that the expression "participation of workers in decisions within undertakings" was a general frame of reference which had the advantage, for the purposes of international comparison, of placing the emphasis on the various types of decisions which had to be made within an undertaking in any economic system and on the degree of influence which the workers might have on the making of these decisions, according to the nature of the problems involved, rather than on the very different types of institutional machinery through which this influence might be exercised.

42. Seen in this perspective, the expression "participation of workers in decisions within undertakings" allowed a comparison of the influence of workers on the preparation, making and follow-up of decisions taken at the undertaking level in various matters (such as fixing of wages and conditions of work, welfare services and safety, discipline and employment, vocational training, introduction of technological change and organisation of production, as well as their social consequences, investment and planning, etc.) through methods as different as joint consultation and communications, collective bargaining, representation of workers in managerial boards and workers' self-management. It was stated by some experts that decisions to be taken at the level of the enterprise could be influenced by decisions taken at the national level, especially through bipartite and tripartite commissions within which both employers and unions were represented.

43. The Meeting emphasised that the expression "participation of workers in decisions within undertakings" was distinct from and therefore wider than the concept of workers' participation in management.

These statements are as valid today as they were in 1967. It is against this general background and within this general framework that participants in the Symposium are invited to exchange views and experience and discuss practical problems arising from the application of different workers' participation formulae.

It is to be hoped that the present Symposium, bringing together people from various circles and from different regions of the world, will contribute to a better understanding of the objectives, achievements, problems and possibilities of the present and future trends of workers' participation in decisions within undertakings.

THE PROCEEDINGS OF THE SYMPOSIUM

The Symposium on Workers' Participation in Decisions within Undertakings was opened by an inaugural ceremony which took place on 20 August 1974 at 11 a.m. in the Folkets Hus, Oslo. The text of the opening speeches is found in Appendix I, below. The list of participants is found in Appendix II. The working sessions of the Symposium were chaired by Mr. J. de Givry, Chief of the Social Institutions Development Department of the ILO.

The first part of the Symposium was devoted to the consideration of different national systems of workers' participation in decisions within undertakings. A series of plenary sittings took place during which the systems in force in a country or a group of countries were presented by a panel composed of participants from the countries concerned, who then answered questions from the floor. These sessions, devoted essentially to information, were followed in the second week of the Symposium by discussion sessions organised around several of the main themes of particular interest to the participants, selected on the basis of replies to a questionnaire circulated among them. In addition, and in response to the participants' request, special sessions were organised to enable a further exchange of information to take place with regard to the systems of workers' participation practised in the Federal Republic of Germany, Yugoslavia, and the Scandinavian countries - Norway, Sweden and Denmark.

In view of the fact that a large number of written contributions were submitted describing national experience in this field, which are available on request (see list below, Appendix III), it has not been considered necessary to summarise the presentations of national systems made in the course of the Symposium, nor would it be possible to do justice to these systems in a few paragraphs. The summary of the discussions by Mr. Schregle, which is included in this volume (see below, page 61), deals, moreover, with the main issues raised and gives a broad picture of developments in this field throughout the world at the present time.

The following paragraphs aim to provide a brief résumé of those sessions which were devoted to the discussions of specific aspects or forms of workers' participation within undertakings and to highlight some of the questions raised and preoccupations expressed in this connection. Two types of discussions were organised, namely, plenary sittings, devoted to subjects in which a majority of the participants had expressed interest, with a panel of speakers to lead the discussion; and informal discussion groups to consider those aspects which were of interest to fewer participants. In practice, however, all the discussions took place in plenary with a large number of participants present.

It was, of course, impossible to have an exhaustive discussion on a comparative basis of the many aspects of this complex question in the time that could be devoted to each subject. This report should, however, be read in the light of the fact that this was, for many of the participants, the first occasion on which they had had an opportunity to confront their own experience with that of other countries in an international forum and to raise troublesome issues in the search for practical solutions. Thus, although no consensus

was sought or final conclusions reached, the Symposium was felt to
be useful in allowing participants - including the proponents and
opponents of particular systems of participation from certain
countries - to air their problems and views in a neutral atmosphere
and, possibly, to see them in a new perspective.

Discussion of particular subjects

Workers' participation in the organisation
of their work (including participation in
cases of changes in production methods and
conditions of work)

Panel members:

Professor J.L. Burbidge,
International Centre for Advanced Technical and
   Vocational Training, Turin.

Mr. P.J. Cardiff,
Deputy General Secretary,
Workers' Union of Ireland, Dublin.

Mr. P. Guillen,
Secrétaire Général Adjoint,
Conseil National du Patronat Français,
Paris.

Mr. V.I. Markov,
Chief of Section at the Research Institute of Labour,
State Committee of Labour and Wages, Moscow.

Mr. J.P. Norstedt,
Assistant Director,
Swedish Employers' Confederation, Stockholm.

Mr. K. Stone,
Secretary, Victorian Trades Hall Council,
Carlton, Australia.

This session began with a description of the method and
findings of a research project which was being carried out in a
number of countries under the auspices of the International Centre
for Advanced Technical and Vocational Training of Turin, concerning
the introduction of "group technology", i.e. the organisation of
work in autonomous groups, in component processing operations. In
the course of this research, an inventory had been established of
332 applications of this type of system in 32 countries, relating to
the manufacture of 191 different products. It was emphasised that
group methods of production greatly enlarged the scope of worker
participation at shop-floor level by the delegation of decision-
making authority on many aspects of day-to-day operations to the
group of workers, and that it also provided a more economic and
efficient method of operation. By decentralising decision-making to
the level of those directly concerned, more account could be taken

of practical realities, while many other factors such as reduced
turnover of staff and a lessening of the need to maintain large
reserve stocks also contributed to higher productivity.[1]

A member of the panel, speaking from experience in the French
metal trade, where a number of experiments in new forms of work
organisation had been carried out in some 30 undertakings utilising
new techniques of job enlargement, job enrichment, rotation of tasks
and group methods, highlighted some of the obstacles encountered in
the introduction of these systems, which included resistance both
from workers and the management side, as well as the constraints
arising from the technology itself. Although the practical results
of such experiments in terms of worker satisfaction and improved
productivity were difficult to evaluate, in the main this speaker
saw this as a positive trend towards releasing workers from some of
the physical, mental and material constraints of the workplace. It
was pointed out that these experiments could, in fact, be linked
with negotiations now under way between workers' and employers'
organisations at the national level in France covering a broad
spectrum of working conditions.

Such experiments had been carried further in Sweden, where,
according to another member of the panel, over a thousand firms had
tried out new ideas in organising the work of production.
Significant results had been achieved in a number of cases on flow
process and assembly-line systems through a co-operative effort of
management and workers in redesigning the work organisation and the
structure of authority. The introduction of group methods in batch
production systems was also the focus of a considerable number of
experiments. The Swedish experience was based on the premise that
in introducing changes in work organisation at the shop-floor level,
it was necessary to take into consideration the whole working
environment including conditions of employment, the design of jobs,
the physical environment, human relations, and the existence of
formal processes of worker participation in the plant, in order to
improve the situation of workers on a broad and enduring basis.

In answer to questions from the floor, the panelists pointed
out that the autonomous group system and other methods involving the
decentralisation of authority were applicable in a wide variety of
different types of production and that experience showed that
service industries and offices were also susceptible to being
organised in this way. In fact, they felt that group technology was
more in the nature of a new philosophy of management than a
technique adapted to certain types of production.

A number of the questions raised in the discussion related to
practical problems connected with the organisation of work in
autonomous groups. The position of the foreman, where decision-
making authority on such matters as job assignment, production
scheduling or quality control was delegated to the group of workers,
preoccupied many of the speakers. Although in the research carried
out by the Turin Centre only one case had been found where the
----

[1] The findings of this research study carried out by the
International Centre for Advanced Technical and Vocational Training
of Turin were discussed at a Symposium on the Effects of Group
Production Methods on the Humanisation of Work, held at the Turin
Centre, 29 June to 5 July 1975.

foreman had been dispensed with entirely - and employed elsewhere in the company - it was evident that the supervisory function was bound to change to an advisory rather than authoritative role, and that this would call for an adjustment in attitudes and further training in some cases. The effect on promotion possibilities of group organisation as opposed to a hierarchical structure was also questioned, although this did not appear to have been a serious issue in the experiments studied. Some speakers were concerned with the possibility that weaker and less efficient members would be excluded from the groups by their decision, but, again, experience did not show that any such problems had frequently occurred.

Another subject of concern to participants was the effect of new systems of work organisation on conditions of work; for example, one participant raised the question of the relationship of such innovations to experiments in flexible working hours, which, however did not appear significant on the basis of present experience. A more delicate problem raised by several participants was the effect on remuneration, in particular, how to calculate productivity increases arising from the introduction of new systems of work. If, according to one participant, these problems were amenable to practical solutions, other participants stressed the need for vigilance on the part of trade unions to ensure that the benefits of such increases were shared equitably among all workers in the plant. Several participants also expressed the fear that the improvement of productivity might be achieved through an increased pace and pressure of work for those involved in the experiments, although there was no evidence that this was the case, since, it was pointed out, workers in autonomous groups were free to schedule production and apportion tasks within the framework of a longer time cycle, often of as much as two weeks or more, rather than being bound to short cycles and daily production goals as in traditional assembly-line methods.

The assessement of the results of experiments also interested the participants. While there was a general feeling that workers' reactions were favourable, and that in most cases, after three to six months' experience with the new systems, the workers involved did not wish to return to former working methods, the effects on turnover and absenteeism appeared not to be significant; indeed, no adequate method of measuring job satisfaction had been devised, and it was pointed out that since no absolute level of worker satisfaction could be reached, continued changes might prove necessary. The advantages to management, on the other hand, were quite clear, in generally increased productivity (sometimes to a spectacular extent) through more rational use of stocks, better production scheduling and quality control by the groups themselves, improvement in machine-setting time, elimination of computer scheduling in some cases, and other factors related to the decentralisation of authority - and this in spite of the initial investment in equipment or space required by the new systems in some, though by no means all, instances. Yet more resistance to the innovations was often found among management personnel than among workers.

The author of the research study under discussion pointed out that productivity increases were not obtained at the expense of the workers through a reduction in manning levels; so far, in the cases he had observed, no lay-offs had resulted from the introduction of group work, any redundancies being absorbed by the expansion of production or transfer of workers to other departments. However, since group technology was proving to be a more efficient method of production, it seemed inevitable that some effect on the size of the production workforce would result in the long term, if and when the system spread throughout industry. These effects would not be limited to direct production workers, for fewer office workers were also likely to be needed. Enterprises and the society as a whole must be prepared, it was emphasised, to think ahead to the means of utilising the labour available in other types of employment, outside industry.

The redundancy aspects of the new systems were of particular concern to many of the participants from developing countries who pointed out that most of the successful experiments so far known had been carried out in highly industrialised areas where labour shortages existed and expressed doubts about the applicability of such systems in countries with a large surplus of manpower. However, attention was drawn to the fact that already several applications of group technology were known in India, among which were some of the earliest and most successful experiments of this nature, and that others had been carried out in other developing countries, Sri Lanka and Argentina, for example. Some of the speakers from the industrialised Western European countries were also concerned with the prospect of reduced labour demand as a result of the introduction of autonomous work groups; they emphasised the need for protection of workers from redundancy, including in particular foreign workers - a protection which, in the opinion of other participants, was amply provided for by law and by collective agreements. No special need for retraining or other methods of dealing with redundancy appeared to have arisen as a result of these experiments.

The position of the trade unions as regards the innovations described was another subject to which many of the participants addressed themselves. One participant, for example, asked about the effect of changes in work organisation on the role of the shop steward, and the possible need for a restructuring of union representation at the shop-floor level. Another question raised was how to deal with a possible disagreement between different unions represented in the plant regarding the introduction of group systems. Some participants emphasised the importance of management taking the workers and the unions into their confidence at an early stage by consulting and negotiating agreements with them, in order to guarantee the success of such experiments and the proper protection of workers involved. Speakers from France and Canada referred to the extent to which autonomous groups and other innovations had been introduced in non-organised undertakings, raising the question of whether such systems could be designed by management to negate the power of unions in the enterprise. This, in the view of the panelists, was not a serious allegation. They did not believe that management could or would attempt to undermine union strength in this way, since it was not possible to introduce a more democratic form of work organisation in an authoritative manner without consulting those concerned. Indeed, the unions concerned and the works committee had been informed in advance in the vast majority of cases and in some instances had taken part in the planning of new work systems, as in Sweden. An over-all agreement on rationalisation in industry had been negotiated between the central Swedish employers' and workers' organisations, which provided for the reorganisation of work with a view to increased

productivity and job satisfaction, along with better working
environment and security of employment. It was pointed out that,
while all such matters could not be settled by collective
bargaining, this kind of framework agreement allowed for a flexible
concerted approach at the plant level, in consultation with the
unions and the workers concerned.

Some other participants were more inclined to emphasise the
importance of negotiations on a broad range of working conditions,
which could not be dissociated from the question of organisation of
work - for example, matters such as workloads, pace of work, hours
of work and overtime, qualification and classification of workers,
wages and methods of remuneration, were all subject to change under
the new systems and such changes, they felt, should be kept under
the control of the collective bargaining process. In the main, the
discussions revealed that trade union hostility to the experiments
seemed to be yielding to a more positive approach, although some
misgivings remained as to the ultimate motivations of management and
the real benefits for workers.

Finally, a recurrent theme of the discussion was the extent to
which autonomous groups or other systems of work organisation which
allowed for greater worker participation in decisions at the shop-
floor level could be related to systems of representative
participation in the enterprise and to the ideal of industrial
democracy. Several of the participants questioned the extent of
real autonomy and decision-making power granted to workers under
these systems, which had been introduced for the most part on the
initiative of management, and where management retained the
authority to set production goals and methods of work. Innovations
primarily designed to increase productivity could in no way be
equated with experiments in industrial democracy, several
participants thought. Others saw these experiments in shop-floor
participation more as a humanitarian exercise designed to improve
workplace conditions and the quality of human relations between
workers and management rather than as a real transfer of power to
workers within the undertaking. Many speakers were dubious about
the possibility of any influence from more democratic methods of
organising work at shop-floor level, filtering upwards to other
levels of management, although others expressed the opinion that the
management hierarchy as a whole was bound to undergo some change
towards a more open and flexible approach to the sharing of
authority, with fewer levels of management, as a result of the
introduction of such systems. As regards the relationship with
representative forms of worker participation at higher levels,
several speakers confirmed that there did not seem to be any
reciprocal influence between such systems, where they existed, and
the success of shop-floor experiments. Indeed, the success or
failure of experiments seemed to depend much more on the practical
quality of advance planning and the adequacy of communication of
objectives and reasons for the change to those concerned, rather
than on any structural aspects such as the existence of worker
directors, works committees, trade union representation in the
enterprise, or other factors related to participation.

One of the participants inquired whether shop-floor
participation could be envisaged as a kind of grass-root training in
democracy which might eventually have repercussions on the basically
authoritarian nature of some developing societies. Although, as one
speaker pointed out, there was no historical correlation between

political democracy and a democratic social organisation in industry, it was conceded that in the long term there might be some contagion from the one to the other.

Problems arising from the representation
of workers on boards of management or
supervisory boards of undertakings

Panel members:

   Mr. M.R. Chowdhury, Chief Labour Officer,
   Bangladesh Jute Industries Corporation, Dacca.

   Mr. J.L. Edwards, Under Secretary of Industrial Relations,
   Department of Employment, London.

   Mr. L. Grafström, Assistant Director,
   Swedish Employers' Confederation, Stockholm.

   Mr. A.P. Kasanga, Senior Labour Officer, Grade 1,
   Ministry of Labour and Social Welfare,
   Dar es Salaam, Tanzania.

   Mr. B. Otto, Chief of the President's Office,
   German Confederation of Trade Unions, Dusseldorf.

The discussions centred around the experience acquired and the claims being made in the Federal Republic of Germany and in the United Kingdom and on the recent experience of Sweden and Tanzania. Participants whose countries had adopted a system of this kind emphasised that the experience described had taken place within a particular national setting and that they did not think it could be applied without change in a different setting.

There was considerable discussion as to whether the representation of workers on boards of management should be on a parity basis, as has so far been the practice in the major steelworks and mining undertakings in the Federal Republic of Germany (which was what the unions of that country wanted for all the big undertakings and was in fact provided for in a recent bill), and as demanded by the British trade union movement, or, on the contrary, whether there should be minority representation, as in other industries in the Federal Republic of Germany, in Sweden and in most of the other countries with market economies where workers are represented on management bodies. Several participants made the point that the purpose of equal representation was better protection of the workers' interests and a better balance within the undertaking between the suppliers of capital and the suppliers of labour, particularly in view of the growing tendency towards concentration in large production units. Various other participants stressed the fact that, while they were satisfied with the system of minority representation in their countries, they feared that equal representation might not correspond to a true balance in representation in the undertaking (for example, the workers' interests were already represented through the works council or committee) and might threaten the autonomy of the social partners in collective bargaining, or even the efficient running of the undertaking since, in a market economy, very fast reactions were necessary on the part of the management.

Among other considerations, they referred to the danger that
a redistribution of power might result in the trade unions having a
dominant influence in national life, in the economy and in
collective bargaining, whereas according to certain surveys to which
they referred, the workers attached less importance to co-
determination of this kind than the trade unions. It was recalled
that on the supervisory boards of undertakings in the Federal
Republic of Germany on which the workers' representatives made up
only one-third of the members, these representatives were elected
directly by the personnel whereas in the case of equal
representation (steelworks or mines), the appointment of some of the
said representatives was undertaken by the unions and members of the
works council who, eight times out of ten, were active trade
unionists. The question was even raised as to which system was most
likely to protect the interests of the consumers.

Other participants pointed out that workers' representatives
on management bodies aimed, above all, at protecting the interests
of the workers - which was what trade unions were for - while
respecting those of the consumers, most of whom were workers, and of
the undertaking, on which job security depended.

Some of the participants from developing countries considered
that the introduction of equal representation of workers on
management bodies in their national systems was premature when
minority workers' representation on the management boards of public
or semi-public undertakings in their countries had not yet produced
significant results. A further difficulty might arise in some cases
as, for example, in India, from the multiplicity of trade unions.
Among the industrialised countries, one of the cases quoted was that
of the United Kingdom and the system of minority representation at
the regional level in the nationalised British Steel Corporation.
Initially, members from the workers' side who had been appointed to
bodies at this level which in principle, had only an advisory role,
were obliged to give up their trade union office. This system had
been changed but experience in this area had remained limited and
for some months now the British trade union movement had been
demanding equal workers' representation by trade union
representatives on management bodies of the supervisory-board type
in both public and private undertakings.

The problem of the possibility of a conflict between
collective bargaining and participation in management bodies by
workers' representatives was discussed at length, particularly in
the case of equal representation. Mention was made of the
possibility of a conflict of interests for the workers'
representatives who would be expected to defend both the interests
of the staff in collective bargaining and those of the undertaking
on the board of directors, thus possibly having to face the problem
of divided loyalties. Several participants emphasised that rather
than there being an incompatibility between participation in
management and collective bargaining, there was a possibility of a
variety of different methods of participation in decisions existing
side by side, since workers and their unions might wish to
participate at various levels and on various bodies, where decisions
were taken concerning them, right from the forecasting and planning
stage.

During the discussion it was emphasised that in the Federal
Republic of Germany and Sweden, for example, collective bargaining

took place mainly at levels higher than the undertaking. Recent Swedish legislation, under which it was possible to have minority workers' representation on the boards of directors of undertakings if the local union so requested, stipulated that these representatives could not take part, on such a body, in discussions connected with bargaining or likely to result in a collective agreement. Certain participants from the Federal Republic of Germany and Sweden stated that, in their view, minority representation of workers on management bodies was not incompatible with collective bargaining but that the latter might be distorted if, with parity representation, undue influence was given to workers' representatives in the appointment and, particularly, re-election of managers.

Some of the participants pointed out, furthermore, that participation in company boards was a particularly effective safeguard of certain interests of the workers, such as job security, and that it could promote information and thus collective bargaining itself. In this connection, mention was made of the fear that certain confidential information might reach the undertaking's rivals but it was also emphasised that this risk was not confined to workers' representation since some shareholders - and banks in particular - sometimes had interests in several rival firms; furthermore, this risk was equally likely to occur with works councils.

Various participants from developing countries stated their preference for collective bargaining rather than workers' representation on management bodies and one stated how impressed he was by the fact that the system of participation in the Federal Republic of Germany did not seem to have undermined the competitiveness of undertakings in this country on international markets.

Some of the participants from industrialised countries expressed their fears at seeing workers' representatives associated in decisions taken by the management body on matters such as retrenchment, in the event of a difficult economic situation, thus raising the problem of co-responsibility in managerial decisions as well as the problem of the possibility of staff representatives being removed from office by those who had appointed them.

In response to a question as to whether workers might be prepared to share the economic risks of their undertaking in such ways as wage cuts, etc., in times of economic difficulties, as a counterpart of participation in decisions, it was pointed out that for the personnel of an undertaking the risk of losing their jobs constituted a major participation in the risks of the firm. It was recalled, furthermore, that co-determination in the coal mines in the Federal Republic of Germany had been of considerable help in coping with the marked decline in this industry, without too many social problems.

A number of other problems were discussed, such as the fact that in various countries only part of the workers belonged to a trade union, which might influence representation of the interests of non-unionised workers and, possibly, the manner of appointing staff representatives on management bodies. A further question raised was whether representation of this kind should be assumed solely by members of the personnel or include trade union repre-

sentatives from outside the undertaking. Various worker
participants considered that the two problems would not give rise to
any difficulties in practice, since the purpose of trade unions was
to defend the workers' interests in the best possible manner.

In addition, the question of workers' participation in the
management of holding companies and in multinational companies was
raised. It was stated that in holding companies it was particularly
important to have economic information and that, for example in the
Federal Republic of Germany, the fact that some of them were joint-
stock companies with a large turnover could make them subject to
board participation. In the case of multinational companies,
emphasis was placed both on the need for information and on the real
location of decision-making centres. Mention was made in this
connection of the activities of trade union organisations at the
international level, particularly through the international trade
secretariats and the world councils or similar bodies that already
existed in certain industries or for certain major multinational
enterprises and at which representatives of the workers of the
various establishments or subsidiaries could meet.

It was recalled that in the system applied in the Federal
Republic of Germany a clear distinction had to be made between the
supervisory board, on which the workers were represented, and the
management board. The members of the latter are appointed by the
supervisory board and can be removed from office by it, but the
supervisory board is essentially a supervisory body concerned with
the main lines of policy of the undertaking and in this context
ensures protection of the interests both of the workers and of the
shareholders, the management board being responsible for the day-to-
day running of the firm. This two-tiered structure is not, however,
found in all countries which have adopted a system of workers'
representation in management bodies.

Workers' participation in decisions in the
field of investments, as well as on problems
relating to workers' participation in the
capital of undertakings

The discussion on this item, which was organised in an
informal group meeting without a panel, centred mainly on problems
relating to various methods of workers' participation in profits and
in the share capital of undertakings. Several of the speakers
pointed out that the broadening of the basis of capital ownership
was part of general public policy in a number of countries, and that
the number of shareholders had greatly increased in recent years.
In the Federal Republic of Germany, for example, this was due in
part to government initiatives in offering stock to workers in
publicly owned companies at preferential rates and tax incentives
for investment. In France, legislation had been adopted with a view
to encouraging worker participation in capital and profits in both
public and private sectors. In the United States, also, the
Government sought to promote shareholding and capital investment
schemes for workers by favourable tax treatment. Many enterprises
in these countries, among others, had introduced on a voluntary
basis plans whereby shares in the company were offered to employees
at a special low rate, or were distributed free of charge.

While such schemes had been more or less successful, more so
apparently among white-collar and professional staff than among
blue-collar workers, several speakers drew attention to the fact
that neither workers generally nor the trade unions appeared to be
particularly enthusiastic about profit-sharing or capital-sharing
systems. In many instances, for example, workers had rapidly sold
the shares distributed to them as soon as this was permitted under
the plan. Some participants pointed out that the fact that share
capital was blocked for a number of years acted as a deterrent to
shareholding by workers who preferred cash gains needed for family
income or for the purchase of consumer goods, and that in a period
of declining monetary values, moreover, the low-interest-bearing
shares were not a profitable investment. Several speakers also
pointed out that profit-sharing plans were generally calculated in
such a way that only an infinitesimal proportion of the real profits
of the undertaking was made available to workers. Thus, both from
a practical viewpoint and as a means of achieving a more equitable
distribution of the plus-value created by their work, these scehemes
offered little advantage to workers in the opinion of these
participants.

The relationship between capital ownership for workers and
their participation in decisions concerning the undertaking was not
evident to many of the participants. One participant, for example,
pointed out that if such schemes were intended really to transfer
decision-making power in undertakings to the workers, it was
necessary for the latter to be able to obtain a majority share of
the capital, whereas under most of the schemes in operation at
present they only had access to a limited proportion of the shares.
This gave them no more effective a voice than any other minority
shareholder. Reference was made in this connection to various other
systems of worker ownership, for example, producer co-operatives;
but several speakers recalled that such systems had often failed in
the past either through bad management or too great financial
success which undermined the democratic operation of the
undertaking. It was recalled that the Yugoslav experience in
workers' self-management had achieved notable results both in the
creation of employment and more equal distribution of income;
however, several speakers noted that perhaps of greater interest to
countries with a free market economy was the experiment being
carried on in Peru, where private companies of a certain size were
obliged by law to contribute 15 per cent of their profits to an
"industrial community", owned by the labour force as a whole rather
than by individual workers. This type of solution, many speakers
felt, would be especially useful in developing countries where a
large proportion of the population was still constituted by the
rural poor, and the problem was one of mobilising savings to finance
development plans in the rural sector. These participants felt that
individual shareholdings by workers would have no significant impact
on decisions within undertakings, whereas ownership of capital by
workers on a collective basis, through trade unions, co-operatives,
or other means could influence the policy of undertakings and the
direction of development.

It was noted that in Denmark the debate on co-ownership of the
means of production was closely linked with the demand for co-
determination rights in the undertaking. The Danish trade union
movement had adopted, in 1971, a programme of "economic democracy"
which aimed to ensure a more equal share for workers of ownership of
capital and capital growth, and, hence, a stronger influence on

decisions. A legislative proposal had been formulated, but not yet adopted, which would set up a central fund, into which employers in both the public and private sectors would pay 5 per cent of their wage bill, to be used for investment in Danish industry for the benefit of small as well as large undertakings. The fund would be common property, administered by a committee of specialists appointed by trade unions. Some opponents of the proposal felt that this solution would prevent workers from having any sense of individual participation or influence and would defeat the purposes of the national agreement on co-operation which had sought to promote worker interest and participation in the running of the enterprise in which he was employed.

Problems relating to the operation of organs
of workers' representation in undertakings
such as works councils or joint consultation
committees

Panel members:

Mr. C. Asplund, Ombudsman,
The Swedish Central Organisation of Salaried Employees,
Stockholm.

Mr. M. Buza, Director of the Trade Union Institute of
    Theoretical Research,
Central Council of Hungarian Trade Unions, Budapest.

Mr. K.P. DeWitt, Director of the Union-Management
    Services Branch,
Canada Department of Labour, Ottawa.

Mr. R.T. Patterson, President,
Chamber of Commerce and Industry of South Australia,
Adelaide.

It was clear, from the account given by the members of the panel and from the subsequent discussion, that works councils or committees and other bodies of the same kind still represented the most widespread form of workers' participation. It was also made clear that although these bodies always enjoyed the right to information, they only rarely enjoyed rights of co-decision, the latter being in any case frequently confined to the administration of welfare activities.

The discussion also revealed that, generally speaking, works councils did not seem to have come up to expectations - which was seen in particular in the fact that in countries where their establishment was not compulsory, generally only few of them had been set up. There seemed to be many reasons for this lack of enthusiasm and particular mention was made of a certain lack of interest on the part of the workers in the matters dealt with by the works councils, the bureaucratic nature of some of the procedures followed within them and the fact that supervisory staff were not associated with their work. It was, however, also pointed out that the relative disinterest of the workers in works councils was due primarily to the fact that in the majority of cases these councils had only advisory powers and not powers of decision and above all to the fact that they were left out of collective bargaining, which remained the jealously guarded prerogative of the trade unions.

Various means had been resorted to to solve the problems referred to above; in some Western European countries, legislation had recently been adopted to increase the powers of co-decision of the works councils. However, reforms of this kind did not solve the problems that result from the dualism at plant level between the bargaining structures and the joint consultation structures, which problem was becoming all the more a burning issue since there were now a number of countries where there was an increasing tendency to bargain at plant level.

The view was also expressed that where an institutionalised system of trade union representation existed alongside the works councils, and the unions presented candidates in elections to works councils, co-existence between the latter and the bargaining structure was justifiable: one of the reasons for this was that bargaining could not go on continually and that consequently there was room for consultation between two bargaining sessions; a further reason was that some subjects, particularly those concerning the management of the undertaking, were in principle considered to lie outside the scope of bargaining and could thus well be the subject of consultation. It was stressed, however, that experience had shown that the only really efficient works councils were those in undertakings in which the unions were firmly established.

Other speakers described certain experiments that had been carried out in their countries, all of which tended towards a certain integration of the consultation and bargaining procedures, in the course of which the role of the trade unions was defined in such a way that the unions were assured of being the main - if not the only - representatives and defenders of the workers' interests at plant level. In Canada, for example, where works councils originally constituted a form of workers' representation separate from the union, the situation had undergone a complete change and the committees were now known as union-management relations committees. In the same line of thought it was emphasised that in Italy the works councils had lost much of their importance with the spread of plant-level collective bargaining throughout the country. Lastly, it was pointed out that in the socialist countries of Eastern Europe the trade union organisations automatically represented the workers in the undertaking.

Turning to a different subject, some speakers referred to the problems that could be caused by the lack of contact between members of works councils and the workers. Others expressed the opinion that a number of national laws and regulations should be amended so as to extend the works councils' right to information on economic matters and so as to provide for the setting-up of central works councils at the level of industrial and financial groups, whether national or multinational. Yet other speakers stressed the problem caused by the fact that the workers on works councils often lacked training; these particular problems are dealt with elsewhere (see below, page 54).

Problems relating to collective bargaining at the level of the undertaking

Panel members:

Mr. W.G.C. Davies, Former Executive Secretary,
Saskatchewan Federation of Labour, Regina, Canada.

Mr. R.H. Gilbert, Social Affairs Research Department,
Confederation of British Industry, London.

Mr. R. Obejas, Vice-President,
Philippine Transport General Workers' Organisation, Manila.

Mr. P.F. Shaw, Vice-President,
Chase Manhattan Bank, New York.

Several of the national systems described during the discussion - in particular those of Canada, the United States and the Philippines - showed that in some countries collective bargaining is the main if not practically the sole means whereby workers participate in decisions within undertakings.

Here, too, participants emphasised the links between their traditions and the characteristics of their national situation on the one hand and the type of participation adopted on the other. It was noted that in certain countries the introduction of a form of participation, which would be considered to be taking the place - even partly - of trade union action, might well cause sharp reactions and strikes. Some speakers considered, moreover, that collective bargaining was particularly well suited to a highly competitive society. One of the panelists emphasised the flexibility of collective bargaining in solving many problems without having recourse to much legislation, particularly in a country with a high union membership. Several participants from developing countries considered that collective bargaining was particularly well suited to the conditions prevailing in their countries.

The problem of providing for fair income distribution through collective bargaining without undue inflation ensuing and, more generally, without harming the interests of the community as a whole, was also discussed. It was pointed out in this connection that since workers were consumers this was a matter of great concern to them, as was their concern with job security.

Another major problem was that of the matters that could be dealt with by collective bargaining and those which were the prerogative of management. During the discussions it was found that in Canada, the United States and the United Kingdom, for example, the range of subjects dealt with in collective bargaining was very wide. In Canada and the United States the repercussions on the personnel of any decision or change, such as a technical modification, were subject to negotiation, as well as a large number of questions relating, for example, to pensions, safety, conditions of work, etc. In various industrialised countries the unions insisted that all labour-relations problems arising on the job be subject to bargaining .

The respective roles of colllective bargaining and of bodies of the works council type were also discussed. Sometimes, as in Canada, certain matters such as automation or new manufacturing processes were the subject of consultation. Certain participants emphasised that collective bargaining must remain the prerogative of the trade union organisations and that there should be no confusion with the role of the works councils or of workers' representation on management bodies, where such existed.

Various other problems were mentioned such as that of recognition of the bargaining agent. It sometimes happened that the procedures for designating the union which, in the opinion of the majority of the personnel, should have the exclusive right to represent them in the bargaining unit, took time, in case of controversy. It was pointed out that in Canada and in the United States, the trade union movement had its own arbitration bodies to deal with jurisdictional disputes, for example, between craft unions.

The problems raised by the existence of non-organised workers, in relation to collective bargaining, were discussed at length. Sometimes, and not only in developing countries, it took time to organise the workers in an industry and in some cases fear of the employers' reaction caused hesitation. There were further reasons, such as the fact that workers might be scattered in small establishments, and the result of all this was that it was not unusual for commercial and service workers to be less frequently organised than blue-collar workers. Some participants considered that only workers who were union members should benefit from the advantages acquired through collective bargaining but, in many cases, unorganised workers obtained directly (or indirectly, according to the situation of the employment market) the same conditions. At other times, the law had to intervene in favour of workers as yet insufficiently organised for collective bargaining or to ensure that the same conditions were applied in all undertakings of a particular industry.

Some participants stressed the fact that it was at times difficult to obtain from the firm economic information that was important for collective bargaining. Others raised the question of differences in levels of education and training between the representatives of unions and of management. They emphasised the importance of workers' education programmes, including workers' information and the effective application of agreements reached, and of the free exercise of trade union rights in the undertakings.

The question of labour disputes that arose while collective bargaining was under way was also referred to. The case of the United Kingdom in the not-so-distant past was mentioned to show that legislative intervention was not necessarily very effective in reducing the number of disputes. Various national systems for settling industrial disputes through conciliation, mediation and voluntary arbitration - which was the most frequent, at least in the industrialised countries - or compulsory arbitration, were cited, as well as no-strike and no-lockout clauses in collective agreements (while the latter were in force) and methods of settling interpretation disputes.

Lastly, the question of the linkage between the various levels of collective bargaining (plant, industry, regional or national) was

raised. In this connection some of the participants considered that
it was impossible to solve everything merely at plant level, seeing
plant agreements as complementary to industry, regional or nation-
wide agreements. Several participants emphasised the importance, in
their view, of extending the possibilities of bargaining at the
international level in the case of multinational enterprises.

On the whole, collective bargaining was recognised as an
instrument for participation that was flexible, dynamic and able to
cope with new needs and new problems.

Workers' participation in decisions in cases of mergers or closing down of an undertaking or a plant as well as in other cases where collective dismissals may be envisaged

The informal group discussion on this subject covered workers'
participation in decisions resulting in collective dismissals both
at the time decisions were taken and when they were put into effect,
in relation to the consequences for workers affected by the change.
Several participants drew attention to the legislative provisions in
a number of countries which required the management of undertakings
to provide advance information to the employees concerned through
the works committee, in case of closing-down of the undertaking or
of a plant or department or other structural modification, and to
hear the views of the workers' representatives regarding measures to
limit the number of dismissals or to indemnify or reclassify
workers. Under Belgian law, for example, undertakings which
intended to close were obliged to provide advance information
directly to employees, as well as to the works council and the
public authorities, giving the reasons for closing down and the
number of persons affected, who were entitled to an indemnity and
other benefits. Similar obligations existed under French law. In
addition, in both these countries, collective agreements at the
national and industrial level had fixed in further detail the nature
of prior information and consultation concerning the effects of such
modifications, while joint or tripartite bodies had been established
to take measures for the readaptation and re-employment of workers
affected in such cases. One speaker pointed out that the European
Economic Community was preparing draft regulations which would put
into effect in all the Common Market countries provisions similar to
those already enacted in Belgium, including the right of trade
unions to be consulted in advance and, furthermore, to have the
proposal to close down undertakings examined by an independent body
empowered to judge the validity of the reasons for this decision.

In other countries, for example Ireland, India, Sri Lanka,
Tanzania, there was no specific legislation designed to deal with
the closing down of undertakings or other cases of collective
dismissal but laws governing redundancy or termination of employment
afforded the workers affected a varying degree of protection. In
India, for example, the principle of "last in first out" was applied
in cases of retrenchment; enterprises in difficulty could suspend
operations and lay off workers for a limited period during which the
latter could claim compensation and if their employment was
terminated by the closing down of the enterprise a terminal payment
could be awarded by the courts. In Pakistan, it was an offence for
enterprises to close without giving notice to to and obtaining
permission from the labour court. In Iraq, the law provided that

lay off of workers and closing down of undertakings were subject to the permission of a tripartite commission on termination of employment. Sometimes the State intervened to take over undertakings in order to continue operations and prevent lay offs.

The question was raised of protection of workers in the case of sudden decisions to close, such as in case of bankruptcy, when prior consultation with works committees was not possible. In such a situation, workers could claim payment of wages due out of a mutual fund financed by employers' contributions, in Belgium. Some speakers were concerned with the right of workers to challenge an employers' decision to close a plant, and how far the trade union could intervene to influence such decisions as well as to guarantee the implementation of legal and contractual provisions for advance information and the payment of indemnities and re-employment of workers affected. It was pointed out that such provisions were not always strictly respected by the management of undertakings and that the works committee was sometimes only informed after decisions had been taken. It was noted that negotiations were at present under way in France through which the unions hoped to achieve the right to be consulted on the reasons for decisions resulting in collective dismissals, rather than only being informed in advance, and to have an appeals body set up empowered to suspend dismissals while discussions were carried on between the management, the works committee and the trade unions; the latter were also demanding a guarantee of re-employment of all workers affected at the same salary level.

Several speakers pointed out that, while measures for the protection of workers were essential, it was unrealistic to suppose that trade unions could effectively oppose or prevent the closing down of non-competitive undertakings, and that, indeed, this would not be desirable in a period of rapid change and development in the economic field when the restructuring of industry was necessary. On the other hand, attention was drawn, in this connection, to the growing number of cases of threatened closure of undertakings, particularly in low capital industries, where the workers concerned had formed themselves into a co-operative in order to keep the operation going. This solution seemed to be gaining in popularity in a number of countries and in view of the success of some such movements they had been able, in some cases, to get financial help from the banks for the restructuring of the company.

In cases of merger, the participants noted that in Belgium, the re-employment of workers in the new firm was not automatic but was subject to the agreement of each individual concerned. In Tanzania, the employer could choose to re-employ the workers or to pay them compensation, subject to negotiation with the unions. The proposed EEC regulations would oblige the employer to take on workers employed in the firms affected, with their full accrued benefits.

What are the best means of ensuring the
training of workers and their representatives to make their participation in
decisions more effective?

Panel members:

      Mr. N.N. Ajaero, General Secretary,
      Union of Posts and Telecommunications
        Technologists of Nigeria.

      Mr. M.A. Dia, Director,
      Asian Labor Education Center (ALEC),
      University of the Philippines.

      Mr. J.E. Domínguez, Director,
      National Institute of Labour Studies, Mexico.

      Mr. J. de Jong, Secretary,
      Federation of Netherlands' Industry.

      Mr. Ø. Skard, Director,
      Norwegian Employers' Confederation.

Although the discussion on the training of workers for
participation in decisions within undertakings only took place on
the last day of the Symposium, it constituted by no means the first
occasion on which this subject was highlighted by the participants.
The discussions following the country presentations had clearly
indicated that recent developments towards a greater influence of
workers on their own working environments, particularly through
workers' participation in decision-making processes within
undertakings, had already exerted a considerable impact on the
practices and philosophies of workers' education, and that, on the
other hand, workers' education had been identified as an
indispensable determinant of an eventual success of the various
schemes of workers' participation. Some speakers had emphasised the
need for training aimed at equipping workers with a better know-how
in managerial fields, economics and productivity techniques, whilst
others had stressed the need for an education which aimed at
harmonising the attitudes of both managements and workers with a
view to improved mutual understanding and a better will to co-
operate. Mention had also been made of training measures aimed at
strengthening the trade unions to which workers' representatives
belonged. Several participants had expressed the opinion that, with
the new dimension of workers' participation added to workers'
education, not only trade unions but also governments and employers
would have a shared responsibility for financing workers' education
activities.

The problem of training of worker representatives was of
particular concern to developing countries where a low level of
general education prevailed among the labour force.

Training approaches, the participants noted, varied
considerably from country to country and were influenced by factors
such as the degree of economic development, socio-cultural
background, political atmosphere and attitudes. For example, in
many developed countries with strong trade union movements, the

latter would be able to take responsibility for organising workers'
training for participation; whereas in developing countries with
weak trade unions, governments and even employers would be called
upon to sponsor training schemes. In Mexico, for example, training
was an integral part of development policy and efforts were being
made to develop programmes on four fronts - general education for
workers, trade union training, as well as specialised training
related to workers' participation, and the concept of permanent
education.

The Philippines also had a strong workers' education movement,
promoted by the trade unions; the work of the Asian Labor Education
Center of the University of the Philippines (ALEC), was described;
this centre was a politically autonomous institution free of
government intervention, which had been functioning since 1954 and
had been attached to the university at the request of the trade
union movement with a view to increasing the collective bargaining
power of the workers through special education and training
programmes. The ALEC ran extension courses and a four-week
residential programme for labour leaders, while rank-and-file
training was conducted by the unions themselves. Workers'
representatives were given technical training through case studies
in job evaluation, work study and labour law.

In Nigeria, it was pointed out, the Government sponsored trade
union education, the objective of which was to create a new type of
involvement and also to enable trade unions to contribute to better
administration and organisation of the workplace. Residential
courses were organised at the trade union training institute in
Lagos and at the University of Ibadan, covering a broad curriculum
including leadership training, economics, industrial relations,
industrial psychology and work study methods.

Some of the obstacles to efficient training for worker
participation in developing countries were noted, for example, the
high turnover of trade union officers in the lower ranks who needed
training, but who might be moved to functions other than those for
which they had been trained; the difficulty for workers in getting
time off for training (which was generally only obtained without
pay); and the fact that unions often preferred to use their scarce
funds for organisational purposes rather than educational.

Participants from industrialised countries gave a brief
overview of the rather complex systems of workers' education in
their respective countries. In the Netherlands, it was noted,
workers' education was instituted both by law and by collective
agreement. Programmes were aimed at covering the training of trade
union officials at all levels and workers' representatives on works
councils, but also included rank-and-file trade union members. The
training of trade union officials was conducted by the unions themselves within specialised institutes, which were financed through
contributions from employers; the latter had, however, no control
over the use of these funds nor the content of courses, their only
say was in the granting of time off to workers for training. The
training of members of works councils was financed through a levy of
one-tenth of 1 per cent of the total wage bill of all enterprises
which were legally obliged to set up a works council (i.e.,
enterprises with more than 100 employees). In addition to the
training provided by the trade union institutes, workers' education
was also organised by people's universities, private foundations and

undertakings. Joint labour-management supervisory boards saw to it
that courses conformed to standards set, although the trade unions
were opposed to any direct supervision of the training they
provided. Course content included law, economics, civics,
organisational science and topical subjects. In this country, one
obstacle to efficient training had been found to be the high
turnover of works council members, but the hope was expressed that
former members might transmit their experience and knowledge to
fellow workers on their return to the shop floor. On the other
hand, it was suggested that there might be a problem of workers
being alienated through their training from their fellow workers on
the shop floor. In the long run, several participants felt that a
solution of the training problem could only be reached through
raising the general level of education of the workforce as a whole.

The Norwegian experience was based on a workforce with a
relatively high level of general education and a similarly high
level of trade union training. It was, moreover, characterised by
a joint approach of employers' and workers' organisations, who had
set up by collective agreement in 1970 the LO/NAF[1] Fund for Training
and Development, which was now the main source of financing for both
workers' education and management development training programmes.
The Fund was financed through a weekly contribution of Nkr. 1.50 per
full-time worker, of which Kr. 1.00 was paid by the employer and Kr.
0.50 by the worker. After necessary funds had been set aside for
common LO/NAF training purposes, the balance was divided equally
between the NAF and the LO for their specific training needs.

As regards workers' participation, it was pointed out by one
of the panelists that both managements and workers were in need of
training. This was particularly true of line management, who were
usually trained in old concepts, the speaker felt, but managements
generally had little training in participative ideas and needed to
be educated on how to manage enterprises based on participative
methods of work. It was suggested that this might be due to a
weakness in the school system, which only provided technical
training and failed to impart the idea of team work; and that
vocational training programmes should aim at making workers more
flexible, enabling them to take over more than one job in the
workplace. As regards the training of elected workers'
representatives on works councils or boards of management, it was
pointed out that while they needed to have a wider understanding of
the factors influencing management decisions in order to participate
on behalf of workers, all employees would also need some training in
order to facilitate their acceptance of decisions taken by their
representatives.

Training given in the undertaking was considered to be the
most effective, particularly in regard to practical economic matters
where the company's own financial material could be used; in fact,
this type of training was regarded in Norway as a necessary
precondition for effective participation. Norwegian enterprises had
also run internal training programmes based on company personnel
----

[1] LO: Landsorganisasjonen i Norge (The Norwegian Federation of
Trade Unions).

NAF: Norsk Arbeidsgiverferening (The Norwegian Employers'
Confederation).

policies, planning procedures, and so forth. Outside training was
felt to be mainly useful for more general matters such as labour law
and an understanding of workers' rights. It was recalled that the
NAF, the LO and the Workers' Educational Association had intensified
their training programmes considerably after the new legislation on
workers' participation in boards of directors and corporate
assemblies had been introduced as from 1 January 1973. In this
connection, courses for employers and workers had so far been held
separately, though with mutual representation in order that the
other side could be heard, but as from the winter of 1974/75
experiments in joint courses were to be undertaken. This method had
already been tried out successfully in the training of members of
works councils in Norway. Experience had shown, moreover, that
shareholders also needed knowledge on internal problems of the
company, particularly in companies where shares are narrowly spread,
and joint courses were now being planned to include shareholders as
well as workers' representatives and other members of the board of
directors. Reference was also made to Swedish experience in team
training for all members of works councils and the view was
expressed that this type of training helped to promote mutual
understanding, clear away misconceptions of the others' views and
reach sound decisions.

There was general agreement among the participants that both
management and workers were in need of training for the effective
implementation of participative decision-making systems. The idea
of joint courses or team training was supported by several speakers,
but it appeared that, in practice, little had been done in this
field, although a few initiatives were reported. In Canada, for
example, where management and trade union training were carried out
by different institutions, a feeling existed that a gap remained and
that there was a need to change attitudes, according to one speaker;
a new programme was being developed for unions and management with
first separate then joint sessions, aimed at improving understanding
and developing discussion methods different from the collective
bargaining attitudes. A participant from India also expressed the
view that both management and unions needed training in how to co-
operate and solve problems, at first separately but then in the form
of co-education. This speaker stressed that training programmes,
including vocational training, should aim at changing attitudes and
promoting team work. In the Philippines, another speaker recalled,
there was some evidence of a change in employers' attitudes since
they now preferred to deal with trained trade union leaders. A
trade union request in that country for joint training had been
refused by management, but, through the university, courses had been
developed and case studies carried out in which both sides
participated and this experiment had proved very effective. The
trade unions had also requested that management courses in labour
relations for supervisors be organised in the university context,
which presented the advantage of neutrality. It was also stressed
that management, especially in developing countries, needed training
to help them to understand workers' needs and motives.

The method of financing training was another topic of interest
to participants. The view was expressed that the Norwegian system,
where the trade unions contributed to the cost of training, was an
ideal one but difficult to implement in other countries where
employers had to shoulder the main part of training expenses with
some government support. On participant, however, emphasised that
it was better for the unions to finance their own training for

participation in order to create a sense of confidence in their
equal strength. Another stated that in certain countries, while
management training was financed independently by employers'
organisations and private associations of personnel management, all
three parties - government, employers and unions - contributed to
the cost of trade union training.

It was pointed out by one participant that if economic
education was to be part of the training of trade unionists this was
properly the responsibility of the public education authorities, in
so far as such training claimed to be neutral and was not directly
related to the interests of the undertaking. It was also considered
essential for workers to have a fundamental training in economics in
order to understand their role and rights in society and that such
training should be financed on a tripartite basis. Attention was
drawn to the need for teaching macro-economics, and one participant
stressed that economic education must have a wider scope than
enterprise mechanisms sicne it was, for example, necessary to understand the workings of the national economy in order to formulate
wage claims. Finally, it was pointed out that in developing
countries, governments should provide some initiative to economic
training since social institutions generally in these areas were
poorly financed.

Reference was also made in the discussion to the length of
courses and the adequacy of part-time training for workers. Here
again, it was pointed out that much depended on the general level of
education of the work force in developing appropriate training
programmes and schedules.

Problems relating to the information
of workers concerning the running of
the undertaking

Panel members:

Mr. H. Ronnenberg, Managing Director,
Confederation of Employers' Associations of
the Industrial Region of Aachen, Aachen,
Federal Republic of Germany.

Mr. P. Silon, Chief of Branch,
Confederation of Christian Trade Unions of Belgium.
Brussels.

Participants at the Symposium first of all listened to a
description of the statutory provisions and regulations governing
the information of workers on the running of undertakings in the
Federal Republic of Germany and in Belgium. They were told that in
Belgium the Royal Order of 27 November 1973 contained extremely
detailed provisions according to which works councils were entitled,
during every four-year period between two elections, to receive
detailed information at a series of sessions amounting normally to
80 hours altogether. Participants also noted that the question of
the confidential nature of the information provided was dealt with
by a provision in this Order whereby information was considered
confidential only if it related to certain matters, which were
listed, and if the employer had expressly stated that the

information in question was confidential, it being understood that the workers could dispute this decision by the employer and that, in such event, the issue would be decided by an official from the Ministry for Economic Affairs. The participants further noted that according to the Belgian Royal Order certain information had to be provided in writing a specified number of days before the meeting of the works council and that, during this meeting, each party might be assisted by an outside expert.

The reports of the members of the panel and the subsequent discussion showed that the most important problems as regards information arose from the fact that management representatives provided the information in terms that were too complicated and that the workers' representatives were inadequately trained to understand the information received. It was emphasised that the employers should, above all, have serious intention of giving correct information in comprehensible terms. Participants at the Symposium noted with interest that the question of how to achieve this aim was at present being studied systematically in a number of countries. They also noted that experiments in a large Argentine undertaking, in which certain information was given by graphic methods and other information in the form of talks with the workers, had proved quite successful. The discussions revealed that the essential problem lay in giving workers training that would enable them to understand and interpret the information given. Participants strongly emphasised all the implications of this problem in countries where illiteracy was still fairly widespread. Certain participants were opposed to joint training programmes for workers and management representatives since experience had shown that those workers who had followed courses of this kind did not remain genuine workers' representatives and, in fact, lost contact with the very people they were supposed to represent.

It was also pointed out by one participant that the information given might entail certain disadvantages: for example, the announcement of the impending shutdown of an undertaking or of part of it could result in the almost immediate departure of some of the skilled workers and, consequently, in the premature closing down of the undertaking. The fact that some of the confidential information given to workers inevitably came to the knowledge of rival firms, even if it was very difficult to prove lack of discretion, was also stressed.

The relationship between workers' participation in undertakings and the possibilities available to workers of participating in the organisation of the economy at the national level

In the course of the informal group discussion of this subject, two opposing viewpoints were expressed. On the one hand, certain participants expressed serious doubts about the possibility of effective workers' participation in drafting and carrying out important decisions at the national level without previous fundamental economic and social changes; real participation, they stressed, was not possible when the focal points of decision were situated within financial and industrial groups. According to the speaker from one developing country, in his country workers' participation in decisions was complementary to the system of

socialist peasant democracy, based on collective leadership within
the framework of a decentralised form of government. Workers'
participation made it possible, under these conditions, to safeguard
the raising of the living standards of workers, giving them the
possibility of themselves becoming socialist managers.

Several other participants, on the other hand, underlined the
importance of workers' participation through representation in the
existing national advisory tripartite bodies which dealt with social
and labour problems. It was pointed out that in Mexico, for
example, two national commissions with a tripartite structure had
been created under the Constitution, to contribute to the solution
of problems concerning minimum wages and profit sharing, while other
tripartite commissions and institutions set up by law were concerned
with social security and national economic policy, including such
important matters as labour distribution and employment,
productivity, exports, vocational training, pollution, cost of
living and inflation. These bodies, it was stated, were greatly
respected by both the employers and the trade unions. On the basis
of this experience, a tripartite institute on the safety of work had
recently been established and since 1971 another important body, the
national fund for the protection and guarantee of workers'
consumption, had been set up to provide loans to low-income workers,
help finance consumers' co-operatives and take other measures to
maintain the purchasing power of wages and counteract the erosion of
inflation.

Another participant pointed out that in the Philippines
workers' participation at the national level was carried out through
annual tripartite congresses with 100 representatives each of
employers, trade unions and government officials. The Labour Code
of the country had been approved by such a congress, for example.
Organised labour was also represented in such policy-making bodies
as the social security commission, the national manpower council and
national training boards, as well as in tripartite annual regional
conferences and the special national labour committee on the
settlement of labour disputes. In Argentina, trade union
representatives took part in the formulation of the Social Charter
which defined social policy.

Participants from a number of other countries described their
national systems of workers' participation which, while less direct,
enabled workers' representatives to express their views and take
part in the formulation of recommendations to the government on
policy issues of concern to them. In Canada, for example, provision
was made for workers' representation in royal commissions set up at
the national and provincial levels to study specific problems and
also in the national economic council which, for over a decade, had
organised symposia, including trade union and employer
representatives, to discuss economic problems, and prepared reports
to the Government drawn up on a tripartite basis. Employers' and
workers' organisations were also free to submit suggestions directly
to the Government. In these countries, it was pointed out, few
decisions affecting workers could in practice be taken without
consultation with and agreement of the parties concerned.

Attention was also drawn to the fact that, in addition to the
existence of special tripartite advisory organs dealing with social
and labour problems, the system of representative parliamentary
government in itself allowed all sectors of the population,
including workers and trade unions, to make their influence felt in
important general policy issues and decisions.

SUMMARY OF THE DISCUSSIONS

by

J. Schregle
Chief, Labour Law and Labour Relations Branch,
International Labour Office

(Text of the oral presentation made at the closing of the
Symposium, on 29 August 1974)

Mr. Chairman, Ladies and Gentlemen,

We have had a most interesting and intensive discussion during these last days. As Mr. de Mel, Commissioner of Labour from Sri Lanka, put it, we have listened to the "fascinating experiments of industrial democracy in various parts of the world". We have received more than 75 written contributions and we have heard from speakers from over 50 different countries.

We heard about enterprise collective bargaining in the United States, in Nigeria and Malaysia; about trade union committees in enterprises in the USSR and the German Democratic Republic; works councils in Singapore and the United Kingdom; parity workers' representation on supervisory boards in West German companies; works committees in France, Pakistan, Finland, Belgium and Tanzania. We were informed about the special loyalties and lifetime commitment characterising employer-employee relations in Japan, about the system of workers' management in Yugoslavia and about workers' representation on boards of nationalised undertakings in Iraq and of state undertakings in India and Venezuela. We listened to explanations of the role of shop stewards in Ireland and arbitration awards in Australia and we were informed about recent legislation in Scandinavian countries on workers' representation on supervisory boards and about Norwegian experiments in autonomous work groups.

Some, if not most, of us may perhaps feel a bit lost in the wealth of information which we have been able to gather during these days. We were confronted with a tremendous amount of material and it will take some time for us to reflect upon what we have heard, to go through our notes and to separate that which is relevant to our respective national systems from that which is perhaps of less interest. It will take some time until things fall into place.

It is particularly in this effort that I should like to offer you my modest help. I shall attempt, in the very short time at my disposal, to try to put the salient features of your discussion into an over-all and - hopefully - coherent picture. I shall try to provide you with some general framework which might facilitate the putting into order in your own minds of the tremendous amount of detailed information which we have received during this Symposium. I shall try to see whether it is possible to draw from your debates some general trends, to arrive at some general conclusions or perhaps even to see whether we can deduce from these discussions some general findings.

I am, of course, fully aware of the fact that the ILO Governing Body, when deciding on the Symposium, made it very clear that this meeting has no mandate to adopt any conclusions.

resolutions or recommendations, and that it has no mandate to adopt
any text concerning future ILO action. Everyone in this hall -
participants and observers - is here in a personal capacity and not
as a delegate. What I propose to do is, therefore, merely to try
briefly to sum up what seem to be the main trends in workers'
participation today, to see whether we can draw some lessons from
the discussions. In doing this, I should like to make it clear that
I am committing no one else but myself, although I am aware - must
be aware - of the responsibilities which I have towards and within
the ILO.

We have all been struck by the great differences which exist
in the approach to workers' participation in various countries.
Obviously, and this was pointed out by several of you, the scheme of
workers' participation in each one of the countries represented here
must be seen within the context of the historical, economic and
social conditions of the country concerned, its values and
traditions. In this sense, every country is a special case.
Needless to say, workers' participation presents itself very
differently in some of the highly industrialised countries with full
employment and a high level of technology, as compared with some of
the developing countries with mass unemployment, widespread poverty,
illiteracy - as you have heard from Bangladesh, for instance - and
a relatively small industrial labour force. Workers' participation
in a country where all the means of production are in public
ownership is different from that in a country with private ownership
of the means of production. Workers' participation in a centrally
planned economy, of course, is not the same as workers'
participation in a market economy. All these differences have to be
kept in mind.

If one were to go to the extreme, we would have to say that
the only summary possible would have to be a summary of each and
every one of the countries present here. I hope you will not expect
me to do that. We have tried to give country summaries in the
background paper prepared by the Office and you yourselves have
summed up the position in your respective countries in a much better
way than I could ever do it, during the first week of the Symposium
when you presented your respective national systems. I therefore
hope you will permit me to look at workers' participation from a
comparative point of view and to see whether, in spite of all these
differences, it is possible to draw some general conclusions and to
see whether there are certain things which perhaps are common, if
not to all, at least to most of the countries represented here. I
hope you will understand if I, in this effort, put the accent on
things which unite you rather than on those which divide you. I am,
of course, aware of the risks and pitfalls of international
comparison, of the drawing of comparative conclusions.

The first thing which was shown very clearly during the
debates is that any international discussion on workers'
participation or industrial relations in general will, to a large
extent, have to be an exercise in semantics. We must first solve
some of the basic problems of terminology. When referring to
terminology, I am not so much thinking of technical questions such
as, for instance, the debate we had on the first day about the
question of whether the "Betriebsrat" in Austria should be
translated into English by "shop steward" or "works council". I am
not thinking so much of the technical problems of translation from
one language into another. What we are concerned about are deeper

connotations and associations which certain terms have in some countries and not in others and which they evoke in certain people's minds.

When considering such terms as "industrial democracy", or using a term of the Danish debate "economic democracy", it will immediately be recognised that it is not very easy to understand these terms unless they are properly explained and defined. Even the term "workers' participation" itself does not have the same meaning in everyone's mind. I sometimes had the impression, in the course of the debates of this Symposium, that certain people, when speaking of workers' participation, were thinking of one particular form of participation only. There were people who used this term as if we were only discussing workers' representatives on supervisory boards. Others used it as referring only to works councils, or any other specific arrangement. There were participants who said that enterprise level collective bargaining is a form of workers' participation, while others, including, for example, Mr. Chavrot from the CGT in France, felt that collective bargaining is not a form of workers' participation. For example, if we take the term "collective bargaining", it would at first sight appear that this term has a precise technical meaning everywhere, i.e. the conclusion of a collective agreement, and that the expression is therefore beyond any doubt clear in everyone's mind. It is true that, to give a few examples, collective agreements are provided for under the law of the United States, the USSR, France and Italy. However, if one looks more closely, one would have to agree that, in spite of the apparent similarities, there are between these four countries basic differences in the very concept of the term "collective bargaining" and in the values which a society attaches to it. We must keep these differences in mind when looking at workers' participation from a comparative point of view. For the purpose of this discussion, we had suggested using the term "workers' participation" in a broad sense, as defined by a technical meeting of the ILO held in 1967. The text of this definition has been reproduced on the last page of the Background Paper which the ILO has prepared for this Symposium.

The discussion has shown that workers' participation is an eminently political issue. Mr. Edwards from the United Kingdom pointed out that the future of the question of workers' representation on company boards in the United Kingdom will be decided at the next parliamentary elections. Mr. Otto of the German Trade Union Confederation (DGB) and Mr. Fitting of the Ministry of Labour of the Federal Republic of Germany explained that the outcome of the present Bill on extending parity co-determination in Germany to industry at large is a matter which is being debated by the three political parties represented in the federal Parliament. This applies, of course, to every country and it is important to be aware of the political aspect of workers' participation.

However, when using the term "political", I do not merely have in mind the interplay between political parties. "Political" has a wider meaning and, if the term "political" or "policy" refers in general to any action aimed at shaping or changing the society in which we live, then workers' participation has a very important political dimension. This is least visible in those countries where workers' participation is looked upon merely as a management technique aimed at improving work organisation at the shop-floor level or employer-employee communications. It is strongest in those

schemes which aim at redefining the mutual role of owners, managers
and workers in the enterprise and those - and we have heard of some
of those schemes presented here - which aim at radically changing
the power relationships between these social forces.

Mr. Otto, for instance, made it clear that the co-
determination policy of the DGB was really aiming at a change in the
society. We also heard Mr. Ronnenberg of the Confederation of
German Employers' Association, who said that the German employers
were against parity co-determination, arguing that this concept was
not compatible with a society based on private ownership and
employers' freedom of decision making in a market economy. Mr.
Pasic and Mr. Kavcic from Yugoslavia emphasised that workers'
management in Yugoslavia which, next June, will celebrate its
twenty-fifth anniversary, is not merely a matter of changing
relationships at enterprise level; it is a new philosophy aiming at
changing the whole Yugoslav society. In this context, it could also
be mentioned that the Government of France has decided to set up a
committee to study the reform of the enterprise in France.

If we look at workers' participation from the point of view of
its general philosophy, we cannot dissociate it from its underlying
motives and justification. There are, of course, those who during
the debate rejected the basic idea of workers' involvement in
management in the private sector. Mr. Gayetot from the Belgian
Federation of Labour pleaded for "workers' control", rather than
joint management by employers and workers. Mr. Chavrot from the
French CGT and Mr. Rosanwallon of the French CFDT also expressed
fundamental reservations about workers' involvement in the management of private enterprises. Participants from the Italian trade
unions told us that collective bargaining in Italy really had the
aim of obtaining eventually political power for the unions.

Among those who favour some form of workers' association with
the decision-making process at the enterprise level, two broad
schools of thought emerged from the discussions: there were, first,
those who argued that decision-making power derives from ownership.
We have listened to examples whereby workers are enabled to acquire
access to property rights in their undertakings, or share in the
ownership. We have heard of profit-sharing schemes, shareholding
schemes and similar arrangements in a number of countries,
including, for instance, Nigeria. Another example given was the
French scheme of profit sharing and workers' shares (intéressement
et actionnariat ouvrier), described by Mr. Dupront and Mr. Tagliano
of the French Ministry of Labour. We had a very interesting
discussion on workers' shares but it would seem that, in a general
way, experiments in this field have not been very successful, at
least as far as workers' participation in decision making is concerned. The most far-reaching scheme of which the Symposium was
informed is the proposal of the former Social Democratic Government
of Denmark which, under the title "economic democracy" proposed that
a percentage of all wages be paid into a central fund to provide
financing for investment. What is interesting, however, is that the
Danish idea of "economic democracy" is supplemented by the concept
of "industrial democracy", i.e. workers' representation in
enterprise organs. We were informed that this scheme is not being
pursued at the moment. The idea of linking workers' co-decision
rights with ownership is also the basic concept of those countries
in which workers' participation in public sector enterprises has
been a long-standing practice and of those which have obtained, or

call for, nationalisation or socialisation of the means of production. The Hungarian participants, for example, said that the
workers' right to participate is based on the collective ownership
of enterprises in their country.

There are others - and during the discussion they seemed to be
in the majority - who argued that workers have a right to have a say
in the management of their enterprise irrespective of ownership
because, in their view, such right stems from the very fact that a
worker works in the enterprise. This seems to be the philosophy of
the DGB. Mr. Parchment from the Ministry of Labour of Jamaica
referred in his paper to the view that "employees who invest their
lives in a company, as opposed to shareholders who invest their
capital, have a right to influence decisions". The Minister of
Labour of Norway, Mr. Leif Aune, said in his opening speech
"workers' participation is based on fundamental concepts of justice"
and that "the ordinary worker invests his labour and ties his fate
to his place of work. For this reason he has a legitimate claim to
have a share in influencing various aspects of company policy".
This afternoon Mr. Husain from the Government of Pakistan linked the
concept of workers' participation with the idea of social justice
and fundamental human rights.

Needless to say, these two concepts are not mutually exclusive
but do co-exist. In France, for instance, schemes for profit
sharing exist side-by-side with enterprise works committees and
collective bargaining, and the situation is similar in other
countries. The Danish proposal referred to before made it clear
that economic democracy needs to be supplemented by industrial
democracy. Obviously, the views expressed during the discussions
can only reflect views held at a certain moment of time. Views
change as circumstances change. Several speakers referred to
examples showing that trade unions, governments and employers have
changed their attitudes towards workers' participation in the course
of recent years.

I do not intend to pursue this idea much further but it is
important, because it is linked with one question which you have
debated at great length, namely the question of whether workers'
participation should be introduced by way of legislation or by
agreement between the parties. Whether a country opts for
legislation or agreement as a means to bring about workers'
participation is, of course, a choice which will have to be made in
accordance with the practice and traditions of the country
concerned. In the Scandinavian countries with their very long
tradition of basic agreements between central employers' and
workers' organisations, the traditional approach is collective
bargaining. Agreements have been characteristic features of
Scandinavian industrial relations long before the idea of workers'
participation became a topical issue. We were all impressed when we
learned that the first basic agreement in the Scandinavian
countries, the so-called September Agreement in Denmark, will
celebrate its seventy-fifth anniversary next month. This is a very
long history and it is therefore not surprising that countries with
such a long tradition of joint dealings, like Denmark, Norway and
Sweden, should have thought of collective agreements first when they
introduced production committees, works councils or other forms of
joint consultation arrangements. Another example is Ireland where,
as Mr. Dempsy explained to us, the Employer-Labour Conference, a
joint body, has drafted an agreement on joint consultation.

Another group of countries which has opted for collective bargaining as a vehicle for workers' participation includes the United States, the United Kingdom, Canada, Ireland and those countries in the Third World, such as Jamaica, Nigeria, Malaysia and others, which have been influenced by the British model in the past. These countries also are reluctant to legislate on workers' participation in the form of works councils and they prefer to leave this matter to voluntary agreements.

But there are many other countries in which, by tradition, the law plays a central role in industrial relations. This is not always explainable by rational reasons. Mr. Fitting referred to the preference by German trade unions for legislation over collective agreements as instruments for the regulation of industrial relations. To a large extent this attitude also applies to other countries on the European Continent, including Austria, Belgium, France, Luxembourg and the Netherlands, as well as to most countries in Latin America and those countries in Africa and Asia which have been influenced by the French model of labour law and industrial relations. The legislative approach has been adopted also by several countries in the Near and Middle East and by the countries in Central and Eastern Europe.

In a general way, the need to choose between collective bargaining and legislation as possible instruments for introducing workers' participation needs two qualifications: firstly, the choice between the two methods will be largely determined by the type of workers' participation arrangements one has in mind. As regards machinery with primarily consultative and advisory functions, it is easy to conceive of establishing works councils or similar bodies on a voluntarily agreed basis. However, it would hardly be conceivable to introduce workers' representation on management boards or supervisory boards without having recourse to law. It is therefore not surprising that the Scandinavian countries, in spite of their traditional preference for collective bargaining, should have recently enacted legislation on this matter. As pointed out by Mr. Lloyd, the British TUC, traditionally opposed to legislative interference with industrial relations, is now asking for legislation in the field of workers' representation on supervisory boards.

Secondly, the possibility of leaving the introduction of workers' participation schemes to the initiative and agreement of the parties presupposes the existence of organisations of employers and workers of approximately equal strength and a long tradition in the habit of collective dealings. Clearly, these conditions are not met in many of the so-called developing countries. You will recall the strong plea made by Mr. Inciong, Under-Secretary of Labour of the Philippines, who said that in the developing countries the government cannot sit back and that, as a partner, the government must perhaps be the strongest of the three parties involved to innovate and to play an active role in industrial relations. What he said is, in my view, very valid for most developing countries, many of which during recent years enacted important legislation in the field of industrial relations. In a general way - and this was underlined many times during the discussions - governments in developing countries play a much more active role in industrial relations than may traditionally have been the case in North America and in some of the Western European countries. This trend towards more government involvement is strengthened further by decisions taken by most developing countries in Asia, Africa, Central and

South America and the Near and Middle East to have their policies guided by national social and economic development plans, in accordance with the policy of the United Nations. During the discussions, references were made to the Second Five-Year Plan of India as an example of linking government development policy with workers' participation. Mr. Kirubanathan referred to the development plan of Malaysia.

However, legislation and collective agreements as vehicles for the introduction of workers' participation are not mutually exclusive but are often complementary to each other. Many countries have a mixture of both methods. Belgium, for instance, we were told by Mr. de Buck, has a system which combines legislation and agreements reached by joint committees. Mr. Kasanga of the Ministry of Labour of Tanzania stated that the Presidential Decree of 1970 on workers' participation was, in fact, based on an agreement which had been reached beforehand between the parties.

Returning again to the concept of collective bargaining - and this is a point on which many of the participants have insisted very much - we must be aware of the fact that collective bargaining has a double role in the field of workers' participation. So far, we have considered collective bargaining as an instrument for introducing workers' participation. The other role of collective bargaining consists in the process of negotiation of the collective agreement itself, particularly at the enterprise or plant level. The very process by which workers, represented by their trade unions, negotiate with employers on wages, conditions of employment and other matters, is in itself a form of workers' participation in that it makes what used to be in the past a unilateral decision on the part of management a joint decision in which labour and management co-operate through the process of give-and-take which, hopefully, arrives at an agreed compromise, i.e. the collective agreement. This point was made very clearly by a large number of participants. We recall the very strong plea in favour of collective bargaining made by Mr. Lloyd of the British TUC, who said that collective bargaining must continue to be the central method of workers' participation. Mr. Paul Shaw, Vice-President of the Chase Manhattan Bank in New York, told the Symposium that, in the United States, collective bargaining is the main instrument of workers' participation and works to the satisfaction of shareholders, managers and employees. Mr. Winpisinger of the Machinists' Union of the United States also underlined the role of collective bargaining as a workers' participation method in his country. Mr. O'Carroll of the Ministry of Labour of Ireland said that, in Ireland, collective bargaining is a very effective system of workers' participation. There were also many participants from the so-called developing countries, including Nigeria, Malaysia, Singapore, Argentina and others, who insisted on the fact that, in their countries, collective bargaining is the main means of workers' participation.

From the discussion of collective bargaining as a process of workers' participation, two things became clear: first, that there is a trend towards enterprise-level bargaining; and, second, that there is a trend towards the enlargement of the scope of bargainable issues. With regard to the first trend, there are, of course, those countries in which collective bargaining has, by tradition, been at the enterprise level. Mr. Nakamura, Mr. Shiraishi, Mr. Tanaka and Mr. Naruse have explained to us the collective bargaining system at the enterprise level in Japan. Malaysia and Singapore are other

examples and, of course, the United States and Canada. Mr. Ukpabi
from Nigeria gave us an eloquent picture of the central role which
enterprise bargaining has in his country. We were told that more
than 2,700 agreements, that is, enterprise agreements, are in force
in the Philippines today. But there are also those countries in
which, by tradition, collective bargaining has been at the industry
and national levels, but in which there is today a clear trend
towards more and more enterprise bargaining. This is particularly
visible in Western Europe. In the paper prepared by Miss Hak and
Mr. de Jong, it was stated that, in the Netherlands, there is a
clear trend towards enterprise-level bargaining. The same trend is
evident in the United Kingdom as Mr. Edwards and Mr. Lloyd explained
in the course of the discussion. And when one speaks of enterprise-
level bargaining, mention must also be made of such countries as
Poland, the German Democratic Republic, the USSR and others, where
the collective agreement concluded between the enterprise trade
union committee and the management is the main form of workers'
participation. It was very interesting to listen to the
participants from Hungary who explained that collective bargaining
in Hungary is, in actual fact, a process whereby the workers have
the right to veto management decisions.

If one looks at collective bargaining in a broader sense,
including also informal negotiations between managers and works
councils or similar bodies, enterprise-level negotiations are also
noticeable in other countries, including Austria, the Federal
Republic of Germany, France and others, where national and regional
agreements are increasingly supplemented by enterprise agreements.
This trend is not always in strict conformity with the law. If you
take, for instance, the Federal Republic of Germany, we were
informed that, under the law, the works council does not have the
right to bargain collectively with the management over wages and
working conditions but, in actual fact, the law is not always
observed.

As to the second phenomenon, i.e. the widening of the scope of
bargainable issues, examples have been given from a number of
countries. Collective bargaining is no longer limited to the
determination of wages and working conditions. More and more
matters which, in the past, had been considered as management
prerogatives are being included in the scope of collective
bargaining. This trend, of course, varies from country to country.
Mr. Hammarström from the Swedish Government referred to recent
trends in Sweden to extend collective bargaining to personnel policy
matters. Mr. Winpisinger explained that collective agreements in
the United States now include such things as the establishment of
new plants, automation, changes in work processes and so forth. As
described by Professor Giugni, collective bargaining in Italy is
covering a growing area of items and he mentioned the recent Fiat
case, where the workers bargained with the management and obtained
the inclusion in the agreement of a provision whereby management
committed itself to invest money in the south of Italy. These are
new developments in accordance with a general trend, which is also
noticeable in a number of countries of the Third World.
Unquestionably, all this is a very important modern form of workers'
participation.

When speaking of collective bargaining, one has to be aware -
and this emerged very clearly from the discussions - that there are
still many obstacles to the rapid and orderly evolution of

<u>collective bargaining, particularly in developing countries</u>.
Several participants reminded us of two major problems:
difficulties in obtaining employers' recognition, and problems
arising out of the multiplicity and rivalry of unions. It was
particularly Mr. Ahmad from the All-Pakistan Federation of Trade
Unions who described in the discussion in moving terms the struggle
which the Pakistan labour movement had to fight during the recent
history of his country for trade union and collective bargaining
rights. We remember Mr. Nair, the President of the Goa Branch of
the Indian National Trade Union Congress, saying that there are, at
present, over 18,000 unions in India. Mr. Inciong referred to the
4,000 unions in the Philippines, and Mr. Husain stated that, in
February 1974, there were 5,701 registered trade unions in Pakistan.

This situation requires to things: it requires, on the part
of the unions, a serious effort to put their own house in order, and
it requires, on the part of governments, efficient methods to set up
objective criteria and procedures for trade union recognition and
the determination of the bargaining agent.

This does not mean that there are no problems in the <u>highly
industrialised countries</u>. We have heard some of the participants
refer to the problem of the multiplicity of unions in Europe, and we
have heard of problems facing some governments and trade unions and
arising from the fact that the non-organised workers profit from
what the unions achieve. There were also fears expressed,
particularly by the employer participants from Denmark and Western
Germany, that certain workers' participation schemes propagated in
their countries would give the trade unions a power which would not
be commensurate with the interests and wishes of the workers and
that, therefore, the interests of the unions and of the workers may
not always be identical.

I am now coming to a subject which you have debated at great
length: <u>the works council</u>. I have discussed collective bargaining
first because it is against the background of collective bargaining
that we have to look at the works councils. Your debates have shown
that the major arguments advanced in your discussions on works
councils can be better appreciated if considered in relation to
collective bargaining. When using the term "works council", we mean
all the various bodies which are elected by all the workers at the
enterprise level, whether union members or not, bodies which are not
supposed to interfere with the collective bargaining rights of the
trade unions, and which are mainly advisory. This applies to works
committees or similar bodies - whatever their name - in many
countries in different parts of the world.

The discussion showed a <u>general disenchantment with the
functioning of works councils</u>. Several participants said that the
works councils had not lived up to the expectations that were placed
in them and had not produced the results which the initiators of the
works councils had hoped to achieve. Many examples were given from
various parts of the world to show that the works council as a
concept is not, perhaps, an ideal solution to enterprise-level
employer-employee relations. The discussion has shown that there
are important reasons for this. One of them seems to be the purely
advisory and consultative function of a works council without any
real decision-making power. While some participants expressed
surprise about the lack of workers' interest in the operation of
works councils, others made the point that a purely advisory

arrangement under which people receive information and may express an opinion, but have no influence on whether this opinion is taken into account or not, is not likely to create interest or enthusiasm. Several speakers informed us that, in their countries, the number of works councils had remained relatively small and their practical role insignificant. Mr. Weerakoon, the General Secretary of the Ceylon Federation of Labour, Mr. Ekpiken, Personnel Manager from Nigeria, and others, stated very clearly that, in their countries, arrangements for joint consultation do not work effectively because they meet with the suspicion of the trade unions. It has been said that consultation which does not contain an element of give-and-take, an element of bargaining, cannot be of great practical significance.

There were also those who said that maybe what was wrong was the term "works council", which not only created suspicion among trade unions, but also indifference on the part of the workers. It was interesting to hear from Mr. Mok from the National Productivity Board of Singapore that they were considering, in order to activate the role of works councils in his country, to change the term "works council". Mr. Dewitt from the Canada Department of Labour informed us that they had tried several different terms. All these efforts seem to me to be very interesting because names often have an important significance in practice.

The central issue debated was how to make works councils more effective. The discussion has shown that there are several possible ways out of the apparent works council dilemma. One solution would be to give the works councils co-decision rights or co-management rights. This has been and is being done in a number of countries on the European Continent, including Austria, Belgium, France, the Federal Republic of Germany, the Netherlands and others, where the works council or similar bodies can sometimes manage welfare schemes or have the right to co-decide with management on certain matters. Significantly, these rights have been considerably extended in most of these countries recently. Obviously - and this was also brought out in the discussions - such extended co-decision rights must not conflict with the collective bargaining rights and prerogatives of the trade unions.

Another way of making works councils more efficient and, hence, more attractive would be to give them the right to bargain with management over certain matters. Such a measure would, of course, stimulate interest in the works councils but it would be bound to arouse suspicion on the part of the trade unions which would see their position undermined and would therefore oppose it. Mr. Varadan of the Hindustan Machine Tools Ltd. made this very clear when he said that, in India, the joint management councils ceased to be of practical importance the moment they started to bargain collectively because they immediately met with opposition from the unions.

It was Mr. Lloyd from the British TUC who offered a third solution, when he asked whether it was really correct to maintain the distinction between joint consultation and collective bargaining. This is, I think, very interesting, because this idea came from a country which, in a way, has been at the origin of the classic distinction between joint consultation and collective bargaining, a distinction which has influenced so many other

countries around the world. In fact, it would appear that the
separation between collective bargaining and consultation - if it
could be maintained at all - would create increasing problems as
collective bargaining is moving closer to the enterprise, plant and
workplace level, as we have seen a little while ago. Basically, it
would seem from your discussions that collective bargaining and
joint consultation are one and the same process. This morning, Mr.
Dewitt explained that Canada had experimented with works councils
for a long time until they found that the only way of making these
bodies, to which they had been giving varying names, function
effectively was to integrate them fully into the collective
bargaining process. This may, in fact, be the solution in the
future, namely a merger between bargaining and joint consultation.
I, personally, have always been surprised at arrangements whereby a
man is wearing one hat if he approaches management as a works
council member and he changes his hat when he approaches the same
management as a shop steward of his trade union.

In fact, what emerged from the discussion was the need to
develop arrangements whereby the trade unions would be assured of
being the only, or at least the most essential, spokesman of
workers' interests at the enterprise level. It was Mr. Ahmad from
Pakistan, among others, who insisted very much on the need that
works councils, in order to be successful, must be supported by the
trade unions. This, I venture to predict, will be the orientation
in the future.

There are some European countries in which works councils,
works committees or similar bodies have been created by law and
people from these countries may say that this general remark does
not apply to them since, in their countries, works councils and
trade unions are separated from one another. I would submit that
the problem is not basically different in these countries. It is,
of course, true that in countries such as Austria, France, Belgium,
the Federal Republic of Germany, the Netherlands and others, the
works council or works committee, or whatever its name may be, is
elected by all the workers, whether union members or not, and is
therefore not a trade union body. However, the distinction between
the elected body and the trade union is often more apparent than
real. With regard to France, we were told by Mr. Dupront that an
enterprise committee can function only in those enterprises in which
the trade unions are strongly represented. Mr. Heinrich from the
Federation of Austrian Industrialists said that, while in Austria
works councils and trade unions are separated, 80 to 90 per cent of
the works councils' members are active trade unionists, Mr. Fitting
said that the situation in the Federal Republic of Germany is
similar. In some countries, the link between works councils and
trade unions is maintained by giving the unions the right to present
their candidates at works council elections.

In Italy, the position is somewhat different because there the
trend is clearly towards the replacement of the works councils, i.e.
the "internal committees" created immediately after the war by the
trade unions. In the course of the discussion, Mr. Palladini of the
General Confederation of Italian Industry, raised the question of
whether it would be correct to assume that there is a general trend
towards gradually substituting the trade unions for the works
councils. It would appear to me - and this is my personal view -
that it would perhaps not be true to assume that all works councils,
works committees etc. will be replaced by the trade unions.

However, I think that one thing seems to be inescapable, and that is to find in Western Europe, as long as the present trend towards enterprise- and workplace-level bargaining continues, a solution to one of the central industrial relations problems, namely the question of what will be the future of the role of the trade union movement at the enterprise and shopfloor level.

When we speak of this form of institutionalised workers' participation, we immediately think of its other form, i.e. <u>workers' representation on company boards</u>. This issue you have debated at great length and, in fact, this question is one of the major problems of workers' participation at the present time in many countries and several participants, when using the term "workers' participation" had primarily board representation in mind.

The discussion showed that a meaningful comparative debate on different national approaches to the problem presupposes a clear understanding of company structures in various countries. This point was emphasised by several speakers, including Mr. Bonny from Switzerland and Mr. Fitting. The degree of workers' influence on management decisions depends not only on the number of their representatives on the board, but also on the <u>role and functions which the board has within the power structure of the company</u>. A supervisory board of a West German company is not the same as a governing body of a French company or a board of a British or American company. It is interesting to see from the discussion that nothing is sacrosanct in this world and we have listened to examples given whereby certain countries, including the United Kingdom, Luxembourg and others, are now considering the introduction of a two-tier system on boards, following the model proposed by the European Communities. The idea is to create a supervisory board distinct from the management board and to provide for the inclusion of workers' representatives on such supervisory boards.

The discussion on workers' representatives on company boards showed that there are differences of opinion on two major issues: one is the question of whether workers' participation should be the same in public and private enterprises, and the other issue is the parity problem.

With regard to private as distinguished from public enterprises, the discussion has shown that there does not seem to be any major disagreement as regards <u>the public sector</u>. Workers' representatives on the boards of public sector enterprises, such as the Swiss or Nigerian Railways or the public undertakings in Dahomey, Sri Lanka, France or the state undertakings in Venezuela, Iraq, Argentina, Ireland, Turkey and many others, or the British Steel Corporation, show that this form of workers' participation has been a longstanding practice in many countries. There is nothing really new about it.

The real issue is workers' representation on boards of companies in the private sector. From the information which we have received during the Symposium, it would seem that this formula is, by and large, limited to Western Europe but here things are moving very rapidly.

What emerged from your discussion as a particularly noteworthy development was that the views of trade unions on board representation in some European countries have changed during recent years. While in Germany and Austria, workers' representation on private company boards has been a very longstanding practice (in Germany it was first introduced more than fifty years ago); it is comparatively recent in a number of other countries. In fact, the trade unions of most European countries had not been favourably disposed towards this formula until very recently. With regard to the Scandinavian countries, mention should be made, for instance, of Sweden where, as explained to us by Mr. Asplund, the trade unions had to overcome internal difficulties before they could support the idea of workers' representation on boards. Now, the law of Denmark, Norway and Sweden provides for this form of workers' participation. In Britain, the TUC has departed from its position in the past and is now advocating the inclusion of union representatives on supervisory boards. However, this is not a general trend and other unions reject this idea. Mr. Gayetot from Belgium said that his union prefers to stay outside the management structure. The Italian trade union movement also, as explained by Mr. Arrigo and Mr. Giugni, does not want to get involved in management decisions. The unions of the United States, Canada and other countries, including many developing countries, also do not demand board representation. Mr. Inciong expressed some scepticism about the workability of a system cf workers' representation on the boards of private companies when he said that the workers' representatives on the boards might become the captives of management.

Involvement in the management structure, sharing in decisions concerning the general operation of the enterprise and sharing in the responsibility resulting from such decisions, is a step which many unions are not prepared to take, while others - of which the West German DGB is a typical example - have made it their policy to fully share in the running of the economy. And this full involvement leads logically to the demand for parity representation as it is practised in the West German coal and steel industries and as it has been demanded by the DGB for all larger enterprises. The British TUC has formulated a similar demand.

The central issue of your debate on this question, therefore, was the question of the parity of workers' representation. We have listened to a very lively and, I think, very honest debate among the participants from the Federal Republic of Germany. On the one side, we heard the point of view of the DGB demanding parity representation; on the other side, we were informed about the strong opposition of German employers' organisations to this demand.

What was particularly interesting in this context was the question concerning the compatibility or incompatibility of collective bargaining with parity representation. Mr. Otto of the DGB thinks both procedures are compatible and he pointed to the 25-year old experience in the coal and steel industries. Mr. Heintzeler and Mr. Ronnenberg of the German Employers' Confederation said that it is precisely the situation in the German steel industry which shows that parity board representation by workers and collective bargaining are not compatible because, on the bargaining committee on the employers' side of the German steel industry, there are also trade unionists, in their capacity as management representatives, which leads to a situation in which trade unions are represented on both sides of the bargaining table. Several speakers also referred to the problem of "double loyalty" and to the possibility of conflicts of loyalty for workers' representatives on company boards as regards their role in collective bargaining. We

were informed of recent Swedish legislation on workers'
representatives on company boards, providing that these
representatives cannot take part in proceedings of the board
relating to collective bargaining and industrial disputes. This
debate has shown that there are many conflicting views on this
matter and it was certainly not for this Symposium to predict how
they will be solved.

However, whatever the arrangement for board representation or
the role of works councils, works committees or similar institutiona
may be, one thing emerged clearly from your discussions. It was Mr.
Skard from the Norwegian Employers' Confederation who emphasised
very strongly that workers' representation on company boards is not,
in itself, a guarantee of democracy within the enterprise. He even
went as far as saying that board representation, in itself, is not
a guarantee that there will not be an authoritarian management style
or system in an enterprise. He pointed to the need - and this point
was made by many other speakers also during the debate - for
bringing the individual workers at the shop-floor level into any
form of workers' participation scheme. And this brings us to the
question of shop-floor participation.

This question was one of the two main items included in the
agenda of the Symposium. However, you have preferred to devote
somewhat less time to this point than to the first item, i.e.
institutional arrangements for workers' participation. But, again,
I do not think that this is surprising because the discussion showed
that it was perhaps somewhat premature to engage, in a world-wide
meeting like this, in an international discussion on the question of
how individual workers could participate in work organisation at the
shop-floor level, particularly if one expects to arrive at concrete
findings or results.

Many speakers referred - in a more or less general way - to
experiments which have recently been carried out in their countries
on such matters as job enlargement, job enrichment, job rotation,
autonomous working groups, etc. The detailed information which we
have received from participants coming from Denmark, Sweden,
Australia and a number of other countries, as well as from Mr.
Burbidge of the ILO Turin Centre and Mr. Guillen, General Secretary
of the French Metal Industries, and, of course, from Norwegian
experts, was of particular interest and significance. May I just
refer here to the very comprehensive statements made by Norwegian
participants in the course of the discussions and to the information
which participants were able to obtain on the spot during enterprise
visits. These discussions and this information enabled us to draw
some general conclusions from this debate.

Firstly, it became clear that this whole area is still very
much in the stage of experimentation. In fact, the word
"experiment" was used frequently by all those who participated in
this discussion. Mr. Gustavsen from the Work Research Institute of
Norway, for instance, in reply to various questions, stated that it
was much too early to draw any general conclusions from the
Norwegian experiments. Mr. Guillen made a similar statement with
regard to France and the study undertaken by Professor Burbidge has
come to the same conclusion. In the joint paper presented by the
Swedish participants, it is stated that there are no standard
solutions. However, I, for one, feel that this conclusion is not
discouraging at all. Mr. Norsted of the Swedish Employers'

Confederation said in his very interesting contribution that we are
all learning lessons and that we are learning our lessons not only
from our successes but also from our failures. So one conclusion
would be that we are still experimenting and that we should admit
that we are experimenting.

Another result of the discussion was that it contributed much
to the clarification of certain basic considerations and to a better
definition of some of the terminology often used in this context. -
It emerged clearly from your discussions that the modern slogans -
very fashionable slogans in certain parts of the world - of
"humanisation of work" or "quality of working life" cannot be a
substitute for workers' participation, although the inter-
relationship between these ideas has become clearer in the course of
your discussions. Workers' participation may, and hopefully will,
result in more human working conditions, better work organisation
and increased job satisfaction, and these matters are certainly some
of the objectives of workers' participation, but they are not the
only and may not even be the main objective. Many participants have
made it very clear throughout the discussion that workers'
participation is in essence a new formula of employer-worker
relationship which has primarily to do with shifting in the power
relationships within the modern economy.

The second lessons which we can draw from this discussion was
that new arrangements of work organisation at the shop-floor level
are very much, if not decisively, determined by their underlying
motives. This point was brought out very sharply by several
speakers, particularly Mr. Cardiff from the Workers' Union of
Ireland, and Mr. Chavrot of the CGT of France. It is clearly a
matter of paramount importance to know whether new work methods,
implying more workers' association with work organisation, are
provoked by a desire to increase productivity, reduce costs, combat
labour turnover or absenteeism, or solve problems resulting from
manpower shortage, or whether they are a direct result of a desire
to alleviate the workload, increase job security, reduce fatigue,
stress and strain, counteract early invalidity, improve the working
environment, shorten hours of work and, in a general way, increase
what is often very generally and vaguely referred to as job
satisfaction. Obviously, there will often be a mixture and
combination of all or some of these motives. This was very
pointedly emphasised by Mr. Selvig, President and General Secretary
of the Employers' Confederation of Norway, who said in his opening
speech: "We believe that industrial democracy in the deepest sense
of the word has to do with the intercourse and co-operation between
individuals who are free and independent and who respect each other
mutually - the aim of the co-operation being to give all employees
the greatest possible safety and job satisfaction and, at the same
time, secure the efficient running of the enterprise." On the trade
union side, Mr. Haraldseth, First Secretary of the Norwegian Federation of Trade Unions, said in his opening speech: "In the trade
unions we recognise fully that industrial democracy cannot develop
until there is some influence at the top decision-making bodies. It
will also be necessary to take measures to secure for the individual
worker more influence on his own daily job situation"; and Mr.
Guillen said: "However, the working man today visibly aspires to
greater autonomy with a loosening of constraints which will increase
his scope for initiative. This need can only be satisfied in so far
as man is ready to assume greater responsibility." Clearly, and
this came out all along your discussions, a balance must be

established, when introducing measures aimed at increased workers' participation at the shop-floor level, between objectives of increased productivity and reduced costs, on the one hand, and increased job satisfaction and reduced fatigue and stress, on the other.

It was also said by many speakers that one cannot discuss shop-floor level participation unless one sees it projected against the general background of industrial relations and particularly in the context of wage systems and of sharing in the fruits of increased productivity. Here again, the discussion has brought out very clearly that, in order to be successful, all these experiments need the support of the trade union movement.

Thus, the third lesson which I would venture to draw from this discussion is that no experiment or arrangement regarding workers' participation in work organisation can be expected to be successful and to produce the desired results unless it is planned and implemented with the support of the workers and their trade unions, or at least not directed against them. The examples of Denmark, Norway and Sweden have demonstrated that some of the most far-going experiments have been based on joint agreements between employers' and workers' organisations, i.e. collective bargaining.

This shows that work organisation is not only a question of experiments initiated by management, but it is largely a question of collective bargaining. Examples of this trend were not limited to the Scandinavian countries. In other parts of the world also, important progress has been made in recent years in the improvement of work organisation by way of collective bargaining. This is a point with regard to which we have received very interesting information from Mr. Giugni, who told us about recent collective bargaining in the Italian metal industry on new forms of work organisations, including job rotation and humanisation of work. Mr. Winpisinger reported on similar bargaining agreements in the United States and Mr. Janzen of the German Metal Workers' Union gave in his paper an example of a collective agreement recently concluded in the Federal Republic of Germany which provides for new types of work organisation at the shop-floor level. This agreement is considered by many to be a breakthrough in collective bargaining in the Federal Republic.

This, Ladies and Gentlemen, in a way brings us back to where we started, namely to collective bargaining. In fact, workers' participation at the shop-floor level must not be seen in isolation, but as a part of a more general process on workers' participation at various levels, including, where appropriate, works councils, workers' representation on company boards and essentially collective bargaining. When using this term, I am not merely referring to the negotiation of formal collective agreements under the law of the country concerned, but the term "collective bargaining" is used in a wider sense covering all collective dealings between management and labour aiming at a compromise solution. In that sense, collective bargaining is not only, as shown very clearly throughout the debates, one of the most essential forms of workers' parti- cipation; it also provides the wider context, the general philosophy, in which workers' participation must be embedded.

But in this wider context, workers' participation must be seen in connection with industrial relations in general, i.e. labour relations not limited to the confines of the enterprises. In fact, the new trend towards increased workers' participation is not limited to the enterprise. In many countries, as demonstrated in the course of the discussion, it is an over-all approach to labour relations in the national economy. The need to co-ordinate plant-level workers' participation with the involvement of trade unions in national councils and bodies of various types has been brought out by several speakers. Mr. Chavrot of the French CGT, for instance, insisted that democratisation of the enterprise presupposes the democratic structure of the entire economy. Mr. de Buck of Belgium spoke of the "joint organisation of labour relations at all levels of the economy". This is also reflected in the Scandinavian systems and in the systems of other countries, such as the Netherlands and the Federal Republic of Germany.

There were also speakers who drew attention to the fact that many decisions cannot be taken at the enterprise level but must be left to higher-level intervention. It was Mr. Shiraichi from Japan who said that in a highly industrialised society such as Japan the most urgent and essential problems of our times are too big to be tackled at the company level, and he referred specifically to inflation and pollution. Thus, links between micro-economic and macro-economic decisions have been emphasised by many of you. These links are equally close in the socialist countries. References were made by participants from Hungary, Poland, the German Democratic Republic and the USSR to trade union involvement in economic planning at the level of the enterprise, as well as at the level of the economy as a whole. In Yugoslavia, as explained by Mr. Pasic and Mr. Kavcic, workers' self-management really aims at the transformation of the whole Yugoslav society, including its political set-up. In developing countries, which have opted for development planning in line with the development policy of the United Nations, the links between enterprise activities and national planning and workers' involvement at all these levels are no less visible.

These developments give, in a way, the answer to a question which was raised repeatedly during the discussion, namely whether workers' participation should start from above, i.e. at the level of governments, employers' and workers' organisations, or whether it should start from below, i.e. the worker at the shop-floor level. In my view, the Symposium gave an answer to this question, which is that initiatives of workers' participation, to be successful, must come from all levels and from all sides, if possible simultaneously. The problem is to properly co-ordinate these various initiatives and merge them into a coherent whole.

If we then look at workers' participation from this over-all point of view, it will be recognised that workers' participation is not merely a technique or the establishment of a committee or other institutional or procedural arrangement, but that it is, rather, an expression of a new approach to industry and society at large where people want to be associated with the taking of decisions affecting them. This immediately leads us to recognise that the wish and will to participate is not enough. What is equally important is that people who desire to participate possess the necessary information and the necessary technical skills to enable them to participate.

It was made very clear in the course of the discussion that one of the pre-conditions of participation was the need to provide workers and their representatives with the appropriate information. Many speakers also stressed the necessity to equip workers who are called upon to participate with the necessary technical know-how and understanding without which no participation scheme can function. Frequent references were made to the need for workers' representatives, whether on boards, works councils or at the bargaining table, to be able to read a balance sheet, understand financial management and know the techniques of measuring productivity. It is, therefore, only logical that many participants should have insisted so much on the need for appropriate training, primarily for workers' representatives, but also for all the other parties concerned, including supervisors, technical staff, management personnel, etc. The very difficult and often precarious role which particularly supervisors, who often act in a no-man's land between management and labour, have to play has been brought out very clearly in the course of the discussions.

We have in the course of your debates received a wealth of information on training programmes in various countries. We have heard about schemes for separate programmes for workers and for managerial staff, as well as of joint training programmes for representatives from both sides. We have been given most valuable information on in-plant training, as well as on training schemes which operate at higher levels. It is, of course, not possible to summarise all this information but, in my view, three general conclusions seem to have emerged from all these discussions.

The first conclusion is the absolute necessity of having a solid and effective training system as a prerequisite and as a basis for the functioning of any scheme of workers' participation, whether it is in the form of collective bargaining, works councils, workers' representation on management boards or workers' involvement at the shop-floor level.

The second conclusion seems to be that any training scheme established for the purposes of workers' participation, whichever form it takes in any given country, must be fully integrated in the general educational structure of the country concerned and must be co-ordinated with the schooling system, with universities, etc. May I just refer briefly to the very interesting example of the Asian Labour Education Centre in the Philippines, which was explained by its Director, Mr. Dia.

The third conclusion would seem to be that, as far as training of workers and their representatives is concerned, the rapidly growing demands on training constitute such an enormous financial burden that it cannot possibly be shouldered by the trade union movement alone; that is to say, by its fee-paying membership. The tasks involved are too great, particularly in the developing countries where the training needs are strongest and where trade unions are financially weakest. Therefore, several speakers - and, in my recollection, no one opposed this view - insisted that governments and employers should contribute financially to these training schemes. However, it was, at the same time, emphasised that trade unions must have a decisive say in the working out of the contents of the training programmes, their arrangements and the running of the courses. This trade union participation in workers' education is just another expression of workers' participation as a general proposition.

*

*   *

I am coming to the end. I think that, in my present role, I should resist the temptation to conclude my summary with a beautifully phrased sentence about human dignity, democracy and all the other lofty aims and objectives of workers' participation. The Symposium has made it very clear that workers' participation is a movement which is rapidly spreading all over the world.

This Symposium has given us a world-wide panorama of the position of workers' participation in law, in fact and in the thinking of people in the year 1974. Just before entering this hall, I spoke to Mr. Ukpabi from Nigeria who said that the meeting had given us much more, namely a world panorama of industrial relations. If this is so, it is a great achievement for a meeting like this.

If the meeting has been a success, this is due to you. It is due to the frankness, to the thoroughness, to the perseverance and to the fairness of your discussions. You have taken every care and time to explain to those who asked questions what the situation is in your respective countries. What is perhaps even more, you have not only explained your successes; you have also never hesitated to explain your failures and your problems with workers' participation. You must be complimented on this; you should congratulate yourselves, those who spoke and those who listened.

If you were to ask me to sum up in one sentence the main result of this Symposium, I would try to say that the Symposium has shown that workers' participation is no longer a question of "whether or not", but a question of "how".

Of course, I need not tell you how difficult it is to summarise in one hour a discussion which lasted almost nine days. I could, of course, not mention every idea expressed, nor could I mention or quote or cite every participant. I had to make a choice, and every choice, by its very nature, is arbitrary. I therefore offer you my sincere apologies for any serious omission which I may have made.

The conclusions which I have tried to put before you had to be balanced and, in many respects, oversimplified. They could, of course, not do justice to all the peculiar circumstances of every country, every industry, every enterprise represented here. I have attempted to the best of my ability to distil from your discussions some general findings, to draw some lessons, to provide you with a framework for further thinking and to deduce some general trends. In doing this, Ladies and Gentlemen, I have tried to do three things: to be short, to be clear, to be objective.

May I conclude by saying: thank you for your patience, thank you for your indulgence.

APPENDIX I

OPENING SPEECHES

(Ceremony on 20 August 1974)

Mr. Leif Aune,
Minister of Local Government and Labour

Your Excellencies, Ladies and Gentlemen,

In line with developments which have taken place in a number of other countries, we have here in Norway, over a number of years, endeavoured to improve the quality of working life. In order to achieve favourable progress in this field, it has been considered crucially important to ensure that employees be given a greater opportunity to influence their own work situation. There has therefore been a strong desire to enable the individual employee to participate more effectively in the decision-making process within the enterprise.

In Norway, we have tackled the problem from several different angles. For a long period of time now, employees have been represented in various consultative bodies within the enterprise. By amending the Joint-Stock Companies Act, employees have now been granted the right to be represented in the ruling bodies of joint-stock companies. In addition, work has been undertaken on a programme of structural development in enterprises as a means of promoting the employees' influence over their own work situation. Part of this work has consisted in experiments with autonomous work groups in a number of larger as well as smaller enterprises in this country.

The efforts to enable the employees to participate in the decision-making process must be said to have made a certain amount of progress in Norway, but we have a long way to go yet to fulfil our aims. For example, we have yet to give employees the right to be represented in the ruling bodies of enterprises which are not organised in the form of joint-stock companies. In the same manner, those who are employed in the public sector should be granted a similar opportunity to participate in decisions with reference to their own work situation. The work on developing functionally efficient forms of autonomous work groups has been going on for some years, but cannot yet be said to have reached the stage of full completion. Thus, we still have here in Norway a number of major problems to overcome in our efforts to strengthen employee participation in the decision-making process. The Norwegian Government is, however, giving these efforts the highest priority. The question of introducing a greater degree of democratic processes in working life is based on fundamental concepts of justice. The oridnary worker invests his labour and ties his fate to his place of work. For this reason he has a legitimate claim to have a share in influencing various aspects of company policy. Employees must be given greater opportunities for playing an active part in shaping the internal structure and forms of co-operation within the enterprise, in developing personnel policy and vocational training activities.

In the course of the work on furthering the right of employees to take part in the decision-making process, we have here in Norway continuously tried to keep up to date with developments abroad in this field. It has been a great advantage to use in our work to benefit from the experiences gained in other countries which have actively engaged themselves in the question of employee participation in the decision-making process. We expect to continue to derive further benefits in following events in this field in other countries.

For these reasons it was with great pleasure that the Norwegian Government was in a position to accede to the request of the ILO to act as host to this Symposium on Workers' Participation in Decisions within Undertakings.

A symposium such as this offers an excellent opportunity for the exchange of information, experience and points of view. In a symposium of this type we are, furthermore, given the means of obtaining information on current developments in each indiviudal country and we are provided with an excellent opportunity of discussing in depth any special and interesting problems of which we become aware in the course of the Symposium.

In conclusion I would like to express my best wishes to the delegates for a pleasant stay in Norway. May your deliberations provide you with all the impulses necessary to enable your discussions to be both interesting and fruitful. I hereby have great pleasure in declaring the Symposium open.

Mr. Brynjulf Bull,
Mayor of Oslo

Your Excellencies, Ladies and Gentlemen,

I have the great honour as Mayor of this city to address and bid welcome to Oslo the participants of the Symposium of the International Labour Organisation.

In this country we are well aware of the great effort ILO has done in fields of vital interest and importance to our welfare developments. We are aware that their work has been carried on for nigh 60 years. During the entire period there has been active Norwegian participation. Personally I have had the honour to follow closely the exertions, as delegate for our Government at a number of the Conferences. In this city we have had the pleasure of receiving distinguished representatives of the Organisation. The most noteworthy of these visits was when the General Secretary Mr. David Morse visited Oslo on the occasion when the Organisation was awarded the Nobel Peace Prize, and our city had an opportunity of manifesting their deference.

It is rare, however, that we have had a chance of meeting organised conferences under the leadership of ILO. I would indeed appreciate, if it were possible, that the Annual Labour Conference were held in this city, in order that the population here in our entire country might have a chance to be closely presented to the activities of your Organisation. However, I do understand that

owing to ever-increasing activities and enormous technical demands
as well as the always increasing number of co-operators, acting in
front of as well as behind the scene, this will be practically
impossible.

We are very happy to see this comparatively large and very
representative gathering here, however.

The subject to be tackled "workers' participation in decisions
within undertakings" is very much in focus with us, and perhaps more
so than any other subject at present. It is therefore imperative to
us to be allowed to share of your knowledge and take part in the
exchange of reflections and considerations with respect to this very
theme. And we need the inspiration created through close co-
operation in organised forms, with other countries.

Allow me to bid you all welcome to Oslo and to wish you every
success!!

Mr. Kaare N. Selvig,
President and Director General,
Norwegian Employers' Confederation

Your Excellencies, Ladies and Gentlemen,

May I first of all join the previous speakers in welcoming all
participants in the ILO Symposium to Norway and Oslo. Since in our
times Norwegian employers have always regarded co-operation in the
broadest and most positive sense of the word as a basic element for
the efficient running of enterprises which can provide safe jobs and
good working conditions, and which can produce material goods for
the benefit both of society as a whole and for the owners - we
consider it a great honour that the ILO decided to convene this
important conference in our country.

Let me try in some short glimpses to highlight the most
important phases of the development of participation in decision-
making in the enterprises in Norway. Provisions concerning the co-
operation between union shop stewards and management have been
included in Norwegian collective agreements ever since the beginning
of this century. In 1935 general provisions were introduced in the
Basic Agreement between the Federation of Norwegian Trade Unions and
the Norwegian Employers' Confederation. The importance of this
agreement is reflected in the popular name attached to it: "The
Constitution of Industrial Life". Over the years the agreement has
been revised several times and always new provisions concerning
widened co-operation have been among the most significant reforms.

A special agreement on joint production committees was
negotiated shortly after the Second World War, but in 1966 - as a
consequence of the importance which the unions and the employers'
organisation attached to co-operation and worker participation - and
as a result of a proposal moved by the employers a special section
called the Co-operation Agreement was included in the Basic
Agreement. In this section we find provisions for the setting-up of
a number of co-operative bodies on the enterprise level where in
principle representatives of all groups of employees have the right

to participate together with representatives of management. The
most important bodies are the works councils for the whole
enterprise and the special department council for the different
units of the enterprise. These bodies have both informative and
consultative competence in a wide range of fields. The agreement
also provides for information meetings where all employees can
participate and raise questions to be answered by management. When
the Basic Agreement was last revised in late 1973, it was decided to
strengthen the status of the department councils by giving them
decisive powers within a fixed framework set by management provided
all the members of the council are in agreement concerning the
decisions to be made.

An important body on the organisational level which dates back
to 1966 is the Co-operation Council with members from the trade
unions and the employers' organisation. The most important task of
this body is to inform, advise and stimulate the co-operation in the
bodies on enterprise level.

In 1972 a new aspect of industrial democracy was introduced
when Parliament passed a law providing for employee representation
on the board of directors in joint stock companies over a certain
size. The law also introduced a special supervisory body in the
bigger enterprises with representation from the employees. The
employers were not against the first of these reforms, but they
opposed the second. Not because they were against co-operation, but
because they considered the introduction of this new body as
superfluous and detrimental to the efficient running of the
enterprises. We still think that the intentions could be fulfilled
better by other means, but after the law was passed the employers,
as loyal citizens of a democratic society, of course do their best
to make the new bodies work as efficiently as possible. They also
do so because after all we are all dependent on effective co-
operation.

A further aspect of industrial democracy has been the research
work which was initially concentrated on the so-called partly
autonomous groups. These experiments have become widely known also
outside this country. The work was initiated by the unions and the
employers' organisations, and it was to begin with also financed by
them. The organisations have backed and supported the experiments.
We are now in a new phase of the development where we try to
stimulate different experiments tailored to the needs and conditions
of the individual enterprise and carried out mainly by the parties
in the enterprise itself without or with only little assistance from
research personnel. The object is, however, the same - to further
the development of industrial democracy. Before I close, let me try
to state some basic principles which we think are of a fundamental
importance in the development of industrial democracy.

We believe that industrial democracy in the deepest sense of
the word has to do with the intercourse and co-operation between
individuals who are free and independent and who respect each other
mutually - the aim of the co-operation being to give all employees
the greatest possible safety and job satisfaction, and at the same
time secure the efficient running of the enterprise. We believe
that the most important elements in the development of greater
industrial democracy are a two-way information process, genuine
consultation procedures, extended educational activities, increased
delegation of decision-making power and responsibility adjusted to

the qualifications of those who shall take part in the decision-making process, improvement of the conditions for personal influence on the job situation and improved promotion possibilities.

We believe that it is a development along these lines which will give real meaning to the concept of industrial democracy for the great majority of the employees rather than the representation of what must always be a very limited number of employees on the board of directors and the supervisory council. Such a representation can also be of value and importance, but only if it is a result and a supplement to a real loyal, confident and comprehensive co-operation between all those who have their daily work in the enterprises.

Finally we believe that a development based on voluntariness is far better than laws which are imposed on the parties. As somebody once said: "It is difficult to achieve happiness in marriage by law."

Let me conclude by expressing the hope that your discussions will prove to be of practical value so that later in your daily work you can profit from the exchange of views and experiences which have taken place at this Symposium.

Mr. Leif Haraldseth,
First Secretary,
Norwegian Federation of Trade Unions (LO)

Mr. Chairman, Ladies and Gentlemen,

It gives me great pleasure, on behalf of the Norwegian Federation of Trade Unions (LO), in extending the best wishes of good luck in its work to this ILO Symposium on Workers' Participation in the Decisions within Undertakings.

In the Norwegian trade union movement we feel very happy at the fact that the ILO has chosen Oslo as the venue of this Symposium, and that it is being held in this building which is owned by the trade union movement of Norway, and where we have the headquarters of our Federation and a number of our affiliated unions. We hope that the premises will serve the purpose of this Symposium.

In our country it is a primary aim of the trade unions to obtain for the workers an influence on the decision-making bodies that determine the situation of the individual both as worker and as citizen. It has been natural, during the development of the political democracy, also to work for the development along democratic principles of the decision-making procedures in industry. In these efforts strong trade unions and an alert control on the part of society will give the real basis for continued development of workers' participation.

In the Scandinavian countries, workers have succeeded in developing strong and united trade union movements. The employers as well have developed strong and vigorous organisational machinery. This has made it possible to establish systems of co-operation within industry, where both parties feel the responsibility for

observing the agreements concluded. It is endeavoured, through
seminars and other measures of information, to develop these bodies
of co-operation in order that they may meet with their tasks as laid
down in the agreements.

However, there is no reason to hide the fact that there are
differences of opinion between the parties as to how, and to which
extent, workers should be secured influence on the formal decision-
making bodies within undertakings. The participants of this
Symposium may know that since 1 January 1973 we have in Norway
legislation giving the employees in specified industrial companies
the right to a minority representation on the top decision-making
bodies of the undertakings; the board of directors and the
corporate assembly respectively. This system has been extended
later to cover also other sectors and as from 1 January 1975 it will
be extended further.

In the trade unions we recognise fully that industrial
democracy cannot develop only through influence on the top decision-
making bodies. It will also be necessary to take measures to secure
for the individual worker more influence on his own daily job
situation. We have, therefore, participated actively in the
experiments taken place over the last decade within a number of
Norwegian undertakings for the purpose of providing for the
individual employee more well-being and chances of personal
development. Semi-autonomous groups and job design are key words in
this connection. By the last amendments to the Basic Agreement, the
Norwegian Federation of Trade Unions, together with the
Confederation of Employers, have declared that they are prepared to
continue their support of such experiments and development work, for
the purpose of seeking new forms of work organisation and labour-
management co-operaiton that will give all workers even better
possibilities for participating in the shaping of their jobs and
their workplace.

Mr. Chairman, allow me, with these words again to wish the ILO
Symposium good luck in its work, hoping that it will make the basis
for the further development of democracy in industry.

Mr. Bertil Bolin,
Assistant Director-General,
International Labour Office

Mr. Minister, Excellencies, Fellow Participants,

I am afraid that you will have to listen to one more speech
this morning, as I will have the privilege of opening this Symposium
in the name of the International Labour Office. With your
permission I will, therefore, give the floor to myself. This, I
admit, is not a good example of co-determination or even joint
consultation, but rather of. management prerogative. I am sure it
will not happen again during the meeting - in the circumstances I
hope, however, you will accept it.

May I first of all thank you, Mr. Minister, for having opened
this Symposium on behalf of the Government of Norway and for your
kind words about the ILO. I would also like to thank Mr. Bull, the

Mayor of Oslo, and Mr. Selvig and Mr. Haraldseth of the employers and trade unions respectively for their interesting statements which we have just listened to.

May I also express the gratitude of the International Labour Office to your Government, Mr. Minister, and to the employers' and trade union organisations of Norway for having invited this Symposium to take place in Oslo and for all the facilities and hospitality which have been extended to the ILO in arranging this meeting.

I am particularly happy to offer my sincere thanks to the Chairman of the National Tripartite Organising Committee, Mr. Opdahl, Counsellor of the Norwegian Ministry of Social Affairs, for his invaluable personal contribution in the preparation of the Symposium.

I should also like to thank the Norwegian Agency for International Development, NORAD, for the contribution it has made to the Symposium by financing directly or indirectly the travel and subsistence costs for several participants from developing countries. In this regard, I must first mention that for 25 participants from Asian countries, the attendance at this Symposium forms part of a Study Tour to Norway on Industrial Relations, organised by the ILO and financed by NORAD within the framework of a very fruitful collaboration between these two organisations in the field of technical assistance. I should also like to indicate that NORAD, apart from financing the Asian Study Tour, has accepted to finance the participation in the Symposium of four citizens of East African countries, and that the United Nations Development Programme has granted fellowships to several participants from developing countries in Africa, Asia and Latin America.

Last but not least, I am glad to say a cordial welcome, not only to all of you, participants and observers who have come to attend this Symposium, but also to all special guests who have accepted the invitation to attend this opening session.

The Symposium which starts today is not the first meeting of its kind organised by the ILO.

I should here like to recall the resolution concerning workers' participation within undertakings adopted by the International Labour Conference, in 1966, in which the International Labour Office was requested to "undertake a study of the various methods currently used throughout the world to enable workers to participate in decisions within undertakings" and to consider "the convening of international seminars to discuss the problems involved and exchange views and experience". The ILO undertook subsequently a comparative study on the subject, which was submitted to a Technical Meeting on the Rights of Trade Union Representatives and the Participation of Workers in Decisions within Undertakings, which took place in November 1967. This meeting noted that, although it was not possible to reach an internationally agreed definition of the term "workers' participation in decisions within undertakings", this term was, nevertheless, a general frame of reference which had the advantage, for the purposes of international comparison, of placing the emphasis on the various types of decisions which had to be made within an undertaking in any economic system and on the degree of influence which the workers might have on the making of

these decisions according to the nature of the problems involved
rather than on the different types of institutional machinery
through which this influence might be exercised. Seen in this
perspective, this expression allowed a comparison of the influence
of workers on the preparation, making and follow-up of decisions
taken at the undertaking level in various matters through methods as
different as joint consultation and communication, collective
bargaining, representation of workers on managerial boards and
workers' self-management. The Technical Meeting also agreed that
the question of workers' participation should be the subject of a
broader exchange of views and practical experience at the
international level than it had been able to hold itself because it
consisted of a limited number of experts from only a limited number
of countries.

An International Seminar on Workers' Participation was
therefore organised in Belgrade with the financial support of the
UNDP and at the invitation of the Yugoslav Government and trade
unions.

At the end of its debates a number of participants in the
Seminar proposed that, in view of the rapid evolution of national
practices in the field of workers' participation in decisions within
undertakings and the growing interest in the matter, the ILO should
in the near future convene another meeting of a similar type in
order to discuss the developments which would have taken place in
the meantime.

The purpose of the Symposium which opens today is precisely to
provide an opportunity for this new discussion. This Symposium is
clearly very timely, because of the rapid developments in the field
of workers' participation in decision making. Far-reaching
initiatives have been taken in many countries, either by law or by
collective agreement, in the field of institutional arrangements for
participation of workers' representatives in decisions. Let me just
recall in this connection that legislation has been enacted in a
number of countries in order to place workers' representatives on
the boards of directors or the supervisory boards and that legislation has been passed or collective agreements concluded which would
enlarge the scope of competence of works councils. Let me also
recall that workers' self-management systems are undergoing constant
change, as are methods of collective bargaining in predominantly
private enterprise economies as well as the relations between
management and trade unions in countries with planned economies.
Growing importance is attached in many countries to arrangements for
associating workers with the determination of work organisation at
the shop-floor level. An example which comes immediately to mind in
this connection is that of the autonomous work groups which have
existed in this country for quite some time. Many other experiments
have been undertaken, in Norway as well as in other countries, with
the purpose of enlarging the content of jobs, of increasing job
satisfaction and, more generally, of humanising working life.

I am sure that you agree with me that it is not for the ILO to
pass any judgment on these changes or on the immense variety of
formulae applied and sought in different countries; rather our role
is to facilitate an exchange of views and experiences and try to
make a new assessment of where we stand at the international level.
That is also the main purpose of this Symposium and I believe this
will be quite a challenging task for all of you.

In order to create the best possible conditions for the success of your discussions and in order to allow you to deal with all problems at stake as freely as possible, it has therefore been decided that the Symposium would not adopt any formal conclusions or recommendations. In order to facilitate a free discussion it has also been decided that the working sessions of the Symposium would be private and that there would be no verbatim record.

I am convinced that this Symposium, thanks to the high-level position and experience of the participants and observers - there are more than 175 participants coming from nearly 60 countries and in addition there are about 30 observers - will yield positive results both for all of you and for the ILO. I hope we will all gain more knowledge and insight into the different approaches to, and solutions of, some of the major problems of today's workplaces. Through that you will also contribute to a better understanding between workers and employers at the international level which is, after all, what we all are working towards in the ILO.

I believe that having these discussions in Norway - a country where so many innovative approaches have been undertaken in the field of workers' participation during the last ten years or so - can only augur well for an open and frank exchange of views which I am sure will take place in the coming weeks. Clearly in an area still as unexplored and controversial as workers' participation in decision making it is only natural to find widely divergent views both on principles and on the practical application of those principles. Any solutions which will come out of the current debates in very many countries will obviously have to be based on national conditions and circumstances, as, for example, in terms of the attitudes of the legislative bodies, the over-all relationship between employers and trade unions, on trade union attitudes in general and with regard to their own role and place within the undertaking.

May I again thank our Norwegian hosts for their contributions and hospitality and wish all of you every success in your deliberations.

APPENDIX II

CLOSING ADDRESS OF MR. J. DE GIVRY

(After thanking the Norwegian authorities, and more especially
Mr. Opdahl, Chairman of the Organising Committee of the Symposium,
Mr. de Givry attributed the success of the Symposium to three
factors.)

First, the very high level of reponsibility in the social
field which the participants exercise in their countries,
responsibility which was in itself a guarantee of the high quality
of the discussions which have taken place in the Symposium. Next,
there was the very lively interest shown by the participants in the
work of the Symposium, many of whom took the trouble, in spite of
their heavy responsibilities, to prepare a written contribution for
the Symposium either before it began or while it was taking place.
The documentation thus assembled constitutes a unique source of
information on the phenomenon of workers' participation in decisions
in countries throughout the world. This interest has also been
evident in the desire for a mutual exchange of information. There
were not many participants who extolled their own country's system;
they were more interested in learning about the systems of other
countries. I feel that this in itself shows an excellent attitude
of mind. Your interest was also demonstrated by the care with which
120 among you replied to the written consultation designed to help
us in organising the second part of the work of the Symposium.
Finally, the third factor is the spirit of mutual understanding that
you have shown. At the first working session, I mentioned that I
had no rules of procedure to guide me and would have to depend on
your good will. The discussions have convinced me that good will is
decidedly superior to any rules of procedure.

Now I would like to abandon for a moment my role as
representative of the Director-General of the ILO and take advantage
of the freedom that has been yours for the past ten days to speak in
a personal capacity.

When I was a young official in the ILO, the first article that
I wrote for the International Labour Review was about works
councils. That was in 1949. Twenty years later - in 1969, the year
of the ILO's fiftieth anniversary - the then Director-General, Mr.
David Morse, asked a certain number of officials to write what were
called "anniversary articles" for the International Labour Review,
showing the evolution which had taken place in the field of their
competence during the past 25 years and the lessons that could be
drawn from this evolution, as well as prospects for the future.

It was thus that, in concluding an article concerning developments in labour-management relations at the level of the
undertaking, published in January 1969, I chose as a point of
departure one of the fundamental principles of the Declaration of
Philadelphia - "labour is not a commodity" - and pointed out that
this principle involved far more than showing a greater respect for
the dignity of workers through the improvement of working
conditions. I suggested that it also meant that workers should not
feel themselves to be manipulated like a tool or buffeted by forces

or decisions over which they had no influence; that they should become full-fleged members of industrial society instead of being merely caught up in its wheels and suffering whenever it jams.

In this connection, I emphasised that, in working out practical answers to this new demand, it seemed to me that account had to be taken of two essential requirements; on the one hand, the need for workers to have an organised representation of their interests, and for their representatives to enjoy proper protection and the facilities necessary for the exercise of their functions, and, on the other hand, the need for them to have a clearer perception of the function of the undertaking, of the economic and social realities which it implies and which it represents, and of the rules - I should perhaps say the constraints - which govern the management of an undertaking in the modern world, whether in the public or private sector.

For it is, I believe, on the better understanding of the respective roles of workers and their representatives, on the one hand, and of management of undertakings, on the other, that the improvement of their relations largely depends.

This led me to a final reflection, which I shall attempt to summarise. Hitherto, relations inside the undertaking have been dominated in the last resort by the search for solutions to the problems arising from the sharing out of the benefits of production. The organisation and purpose of production has usually played a subordinate part in relations between employers and workers. Without overlooking the need for a fairer distribution, has the time not come to give more thought to machinery for associating everyone more closely with the control of production so as to adapt it to the needs of the community as a whole and to the requirements of balanced economic and social development - balanced, that is, not only nationally but internationally? It is surely significant that whereas in the Preamble to the ILO Constitution, 50 years ago, peace was defined in terms of "justice" - "whereas universal and lasting peace can be established only if it is based upon social justice" - it is now defined in terms of "development". There is nothing surprising about this, for development is regarded in most countries today as an essential precondition of justice.

Accordingly, the undertaking, as the key factor in development, appears to take on a new dignity as the means for the promotion of greater justice. It is no longer merely a source of profits to be shared out in the fairest way but also an instrument for achieving the progress of the greatest number in the interest of the nation and indeed of the whole world. And I wondered whether this mission now attributed to undertakings would not be bound to have repercussions on the pattern of relations among the people who are engaged within them in the task of production.

Of course, an essential aspect of relations within the under- taking will always be to ensure that the benefits of production are distributed fairly, and one of the key functions of the workers' representatives will therefore always be to see - by contractual means - that the workers' interests as regards job security, working conditions and wages are properly safeguarded. But at a time when international economic links are growing, common markets are being formed, undertakings are merging or forging links across frontiers, and the needs of the developing countries are nagging at the conscience of men - all men, whether politicians, employers or workers - it is surely important that the workers' voice should be heard - by means of a supervisory procedure - in the bodies where production policy is decided. The aim should be not only to protect the interests of the workers in the plants concerned but to reflect the general interests of all workers, so as to help to guide economic activity along the course that is considered the best and to build a juster human society.

In the countries where there is economic and social planning, the workers' voice is already heard in policy-making bodies at the national level. But if this voice is to carry its full weight, should it not be reinforced by experience acquired in undertakings, and especially in large-scale undertakings? Despite the major difficulties in the way of putting these ideas into effect - as regards the machinery required, the change in attitudes entailed and the training effort needed - it would not be surprising if the search for answers to these questions became a key factor in relations between employers and workers in undertakings between now and the end of the century.[1]

What has happened during the past five years since these lines were written? In 1971, the International Labour Conference adopted the Convention on the protection of workers' representatives in undertakings and the facilities accorded to them. In several industrialised countries, the question of the ultimate purpose of economic growth has been raised with increasing persistence; and the debates at this Symposium, the confrontation of experience which has taken place here, have, I believe, amply demonstrated that the aspiration towards greater participation of workers in decisions has not only remained a lively issue but has also resulted in important developments of a legislative or contractual nature in recent years.

I am therefore reassured concerning my earlier reflections and the prediction I was bold enough to make.

Now, returning to my role as representative of the Director-General, I would like to say that, from the point of view of the future action of the ILO, I draw three main lessons from this Symposium: the first is that a symposium of this nature forms part of the resources which the ILO has at its disposal in order to fulfil one of its essential tasks, that of promoting an exchange of information. At the present time, it is not only through publications that information is spread, but by arranging for those responsible for social policy, whether they come from government, employers' or workers' circles, to meet in a framework which gives them a chance to communicate their experience directly one to another.

The second lesson is that, as you have emphasised, the realm of workers' participation is evolving very rapidly and it is necessary to examine the situation at repeated intervals, as the European Regional Conference is requested in fact. But, in addition to international symposia such as this one, there is also room for regional meetings which would help to define more precisely the specific economic and social reality of one region of the world.

----

[1] Cf. Jean de Givry, "Developments in labour-management relations in the undertaking", International Labour Review, Vol. 99, No. 1, January 1969.

        Finally, however important the theme of workers' participation
in decisions within undertakings is, I believe that we should beware
of the temptation to try to examine all the problems of social
policy under this heading, even if only because of the ambiguity of
the term "participation" which several of you have underlined in the
course of the discussions. In this connection, you may perhaps be
aware that one of the main preoccupations of the new Director-
General of the ILO, Mr. Blanchard, is the question of the
humanisation of work and the improvement of working conditions; and
I do not think I am giving away any secret in telling you that the
report which he intends to submit to the next session of the
International Labour Conference, in June 1975, will be devoted
precisely to the problems of man in his working environment.

APPENDIX III

LIST OF PARTICIPANTS, OBSERVERS AND SECRETARIAT

ALGERIA

M. M. AISSANI,
Conseiller,
Conseil national économique et social,
4 route des Canons,
ALGER

M. M.A. CHERIEF,
Chargé de Mission,
Ministère du Travail et des Affaires Sociales,
28 Rue Hassiba Ben Bouali,
ALGER

ARGENTINA

Sr. O. VILAS FIGALLO,
Miembro del Comité de Autogestión,
Servicios Electricos del Gran Buenos Aires,
Paséo Colón 171, 8°,
BUENOS AIRES

AUSTRALIA

Mr. J.A.J. CAINE,
First Assistant Secretary,
Australian Department of Labour and Immigration,
PO Box 2817AA, GPO,
MELBOURNE, Victoria 3001

Mr. R.T. PATTERSON,
President,
Chamber of Commerce and Industry of South Australia,
Industry House,
12 Pirie Street,
ADELAIDE, South Australia, 5000.

Mr. K. STONE,
Secretary,
Victorian Trades Hall Council,
Trades Hall, corner of Victoria and Lygan Streets,
CARLTON SOUTH 3053

AUSTRIA

Mr. J. CERNY,
Ccunsellor,
Federal Chamber of Workers of Austria,
1041 VIENNA
Prinz Fugen-Strasse 20-28,

Mr. G. HEINRICH,
Ccunsellor,
Federation of Austrian Industrialists,
Schwarzenbergplatz 4,
1031 VIENNA

Mr. G. KLEIN,
Chief of Section,
Federal Ministry of Social Administration,
1010 VIENNA
Stubenring 1,

Mr. M. MAYR,
Ccunsellor,
Austrian Federal Chamber of Commerce,
1011 VIENNA
Stubenring 12,

BANGLADESH

Mrs. AZRA ALI (Professor), MP,
President, Business and Professional Women's Hostel,
25/A Tipusultan Road,
DACCA

Mr. M.R. CHOWDHURY,
Chief Labour Officer,
Bangladesh Jute Industries Corporation,
Adamjee Court,
Motijheel c/a,
DACCA

Mr. G. MORTUJA,
Registrar of Trade Unions,
Government of the Republic of Bangladesh,
42/43 Purana Paltan,
DACCA 2

BELGIUM

M. R. DE BUCK,
Directeur d'Administration,
Ministère de l'Emploi et du Travail,
rue Belliard, 53,
B - 1040 BRUXELLES

M. J. GAYETOT,
Secrétaire National,
Fédération Générale du Travail de Belgique,
42, rue Haute,
1000 BRUXELLES

M. D. DE NORRE,
Conseiller responsable du Service Emploi et Formation,
Fédération des Entreprises de Belgique,
rue Ravenstein, 4,
1000 BRUXELLES

M. P. SILON,
Responsable National pour le Service "Entreprise",
Confédération des Syndicats Chrétiens de Belgique,
Krevelhoek 19,
9410 ERPE

CANADA

The Hon. G.T. SNYDER,
Minister,
Saskatchewan Department of Labour,
Legislative Building,
REGINA, Saskatchewan

Mr. R.W. MITCHELL,
Deputy Minister,
Saskatchewan Department of Labour,
2350 Albert Street,
REGINA, Saskatchewan

Mr. W.G. DAVIES,
Former Executive Secretary,
Saskatchewan Federation of Labour,
2272 Montague Street,
REGINA, Saskatchewan

Mr. K.P. DEWITT,
Director of the Union-Management Services Branch,
Canada Department of Labour,
Room 1370 D,
Sir Wilfred Laurier Bldg.,
340 Laurier Avenue West,
OTTAWA, Ontario, K1A 0J2

Mr. P. KOZICKY,
Manager,
Ground Engineering Limited,
415 - 7th Avenue,
REGINA, Saskatchewan

Mr. R.P. RIGGIN,
Vice-President for Corporate Relations,
Noranda Mines Limited,
P.O. Box 45,
Commerce Court West,
TORONTO, Ontario M5L 1B6

DENMARK

Mr. B. BORDRUP,
The National Confederation of Danish Trade Unions,
Rosenørns Allé 14,
1970 COPENHAGEN V

Mr. M. FENGER,
Secretary, cand.jur.,
Ministry of Labour,
Laksegede 19,
1063 COPENHAGEN K

Mr. P. ROOS,
Head of Division,
Danish Employers' Confederation,
Vester Voldgade 113,
1503 COPENHAGEN V

FINLAND

Miss T. HALONEN, Ll.B.,
Parliamentary Secretary to the Prime Minister,
Pengerkatu 4 B 28,
00530 HELSINKI 53

Mr. H. JOUSTIE,
Inspector in Chief,
Ministry of Finance,
Järjestelyosasto,
Aleksanterinkatu 36 B,
00100 HELSINKI 10

Mr. M. SALMENPERA,
Cabinet Secretary,
Ministry of Social Affairs and Health,
Snellmanninkatu 4-6,
00170 HELSINKI 17

Mr. T. SAUKKONEN,
Adviser on Participation and Industrial Democracy,
Finnish Employers' Confederation,
Eteläranta 10,
00130 HELSINKI 13

Mr. O. TAMMINEN,
Adviser on Personnel Policy,
Confederation of Commerce Employers,
Eteläranta 10,
00130 HELSINKI 13

FRANCE

M. L. CHAVROT,
Secrétaire de la Commission du Service de l'Action
   Revendicative et de la Politique Contractuelle,
Confédération Générale du Travail,
213, rue La Fayette,
75.480 PARIS CEDEX 10

M. J. DUPRONT,
Ministère du Travail,
1, place Fontenoy,
75.007 PARIS

M. P. GUILLEN,
Secrétaire Général adjoint,
Conseil National du Patronat Français,
56, Avenue de Wagram,
75.017 PARIS

M. P. ROSANWALLON,
Secrétaire Confédéral,
Confédération Française Démocratique du Travail,
26, rue de Montholon,
75.009 PARIS

M. J. RIBADEAU DUMAS,
Président de la Commission des Rapports Sociaux,
  dans l'Entreprise,
Conseil National du Patronat Français,
56, Avenue de Wagram,
75-017 PARIS

M. L. TAGLIANA,
Chef de la Division des Etudes du Service Interministériel
  de l'Intéressement et de la Participation,
Ministère du Travail,
place Fontenoy,
PARIS

GERMANY, DEMOCRATIC REPUBLIC OF

Mr. R. SOMMER,
Member of the Presidium of the National Executive Committee,
Free German Confederation of Trade Unions,
Fritz-Heckert-Strasse 70,
BERLIN 102

Mrs. D. LEHMANN,
Worker of the National Executive Committee,
Free German Confederation of Trade Unions,
Fritz-Heckert-Strasse 70,
BERLIN 102

GERMANY, FEDERAL REPUBLIC OF

Mr. K. FITTING,
Ministerial Director,
Federal Ministry of Labour and Social Affairs,
53 BONN TANNENBUSCH,
An der Düne 1

Mr. W. HEINTZELER,
Member of the Supervisory Board,
Badische Anilin- und Sodafabrik AG - BASF,
D-6700 LUDWIGSHAFEN

Mr. K.H. JANZEN,
Member of the Executive Board,
Metalworkers' Union,
6 FRANKFURT/MAIN,
Wilhelm Leuschner-Strasse 79-58

Mr. B. OTTO,
Chief of the President's Office,
German Confederation of Trade Unions,
4000 DUSSELDORF 1,
Postfach 2601

Mr. H. RONNENBERG,
Managing Director,
Confederation of Employers' Association of the
  Industrial Region of Aachen,
D 51 AACHEN,
Postfach 1626

GUYANA

Mr. P.M.A. BENJAMIN,
General Secretary,
Guyana Mine Workers' Union,
71 Stone Avenue,
Campbelville,
GREATER GEORGETOWN

Mr. H.B. DAVIS,
Personnel Director,
Bookers Sugar Estates Ltd.,
22 Church Street,
GEORGETOWN

Mr. E.A. ROBERTS,
Industrial Relations Officer,
Guyana State Corporation,
12 Pike Street,
Kitty, GREATER GEORGETOWN

Mr. P.A. THOMPSON,
Chairman,
Guyana Bauxite Company Limited,
P.O. Box 7,
GEORGETOWN

HONG KONG

Mr. D.S.T. CHAN,
  Labour Department,
  99 Queensway,
  HONG KONG

HUNGARY

M. F. BOGNAR,
Chef-Adjoint de Département,
Conseil Central des Syndicats Hongrois,
1415 BUDAPEST VI,
Dózsa György ut 84/b

M. M. BUZA,
Directeur de l'Institut Syndical de Recherches Théoriques,
Conseil Central des Syndicats Hongrois,
1415 BUDAPEST VI,
Dózsa György ut 84/b

M. K. HERCZEG,
Secrétaire,
Conseil Central des Syndicats Hongrois,
1415 BUDAPEST VI,
Dózsa György ut 84/b

M. J. HUNEK,
Interprète,
Conseil Central des Syndicats Hongrois,
1415 BUDAPEST VI,
Dózsa György ut 84/b

INDIA

Mr. S.C. AGGARWAL,
Vice President,
Bharat Steel Tubes Ltd.,
Allahabad Bank Building,
17 Parliament Street,
NEW DELHI

Mr. N.N. CHATTERJEE,
Consultant in Personnel Management and Industrial Relations,
Indian Institute of Management,
D2 29-31 Probyn Road,
(Chatra Marg) NEW DELHI 7

Mr. M. NAIR,
President,
Indian National Trade Union Congress, Goa Branch,
PO Box 87,
VASCO-da-GAMA, GOA

Mr. M.S. KRISHNAN,
Vice-President,
All India Trade Union Congress,
53 Gayatridevi Part Extension,
BANGALORE 3

Mr. T.S. SANKARAN,
Joint Secretary,
Department of Labour and Employment,
Shram Shakti Bhavan,
Rafi Marg,
NEW DELHI

Mr. N.M. VAKIL,
Secretary,
Employers' Federation of India,
Army and Navy Building,
148 Mahatma Gandhi Road,
BOMBAY 1

Mr. M.S.S. VARADAN,
Chief of Organisation Development,
Hindustan Machine Tools Ltd.,
BANGALORE 31

INDONESIA

    Mr. CHAERUDDIN,
    Labor-Relations Division,
    Directorate-General for Oil and Nat. Gas,
    Jal. Merdeka Selatan 18,
    JAKARTA

    Mr. DARMOWARDOJO,
    Second Chairman,
    PUSPI (Employers' Association in Indonesia),
    Djalan Kebon Binatang V/3B,
    JAKARTA

    Mr. McANNAS,
    Member of the Executive Board,
    FBSI (All Indonesian Labour Federation),
    Tanah Abang Tiga 25-A,
    JAKARTA

    Mr. SURJANATAKUSUMA,
    Director of Workers' Education and Social Security,
    Ministry of Manpower, Transmigration and Co-operatives,
    L.H. Agus Salim,
    JAKARTA

IRAQ

    Mr. S. ALBAYATI,
    Member of the Executive Bureau,
    The General Federation of Trade Unions of Iraq,
    Abu Nawas Street,
    P.O. Box (3049),
    BAGHDAD

    Mr. H. ATIYAH,
    Chairman,
    General Union of Mechanical Industries Workers,
    Abu Nawas Street,
    P.O. Box (3049),
    BAGHDAD

IRELAND

    Mr. M. AHERNE,
    Assistant Principal Officer,
    Department of Labour,
    Mespil Road,
    DUBLIN 4

    Mr. P.J. CARDIFF,
    Deputy General Secretary,
    Workers' Union of Ireland,
    29 Parnell Square,
    DUBLIN 1

Mr. G.F. DEMPSEY,
Divisional Secretary,
Federated Union of Employers,
8, Fitzwilliam Place,
DUBLIN 2

Mr. N. GREENE,
Personal Assistant on Industrial Affairs to the
   Minister for Labour,
Department of Labour,
Mespil Road,
DUBLIN 4

Mr. T. O'CARROLL,
Secretary,
Department of Labour,
DUBLIN 4

Mr. O'RIORDAN,
Research Officer,
Irish Transport and General Workers' Union,
10 Palmerston Park,
DUBLIN 6

ISRAEL

Mr. B.J. DWORSKY,
Scandinavian Representative,
General Federation of Labour in Israel (Histadrut),
Stortingsgt. 8,
OSLO 1

ITALY

M. G. ARRIGO,
Représentant,
Fédération CGIL-CISL-UIL,
Via Sicilia,
ROME

M. G. GUIGNI,
Professeur ordinaire de Droit du Travail,
Université de Bari,
BARI

M. G. FORLENZA,
Chef du Service "Problèmes internationaux du Travail",
Ministère du Travail,
Via Flavia 6,
ROME

M. E. PALLADINI,
Chef du Service "Problèmes Généraux du Travail",
Confédération Générale de l'Industrie Italienne,
Viale dell'Astronomia,
EUR-ROME

JAMAICA

    Miss M. KENRICK,
    Secretary,
    Jamaica Employers' Federation,
    2A Ruthven Road,
    KINGSTON 10

    Mr. E.M. PARCHMENT,
    Director of Industrial Relations,
    Ministry of Labour and Employment,
    110 East Street,
    KINGSTON

JAPAN

    Mr. T. NAKAMURA,
    First Secretary,
    Permanent Delegation of Japan to the Organisation
      for Economic Co-operation and Development,
    7, Avenue Hoche,
    75008 PARIS

    Mr. T. NARUSE,
    Manager of the Wage and Economic Department,
    Japan Federation of Employers' Associations (NIKKEIREN),
    c/o Nihon Kogyo Club Bldg.,
    4-6 Marunouchi 1-chome,
    Chiyoda-Ku,
    TOKYO 100

    Mr. T. SHIRAISHI,
    Member of the Executive Council,
    National Federation of Industrial Organizations (SHINSAMBETSU),
    Takahashi Building,
    3-9-7 Nishi Shimbashi, 3-chome,
    Minato-ku,
    TOKYO

    Mr. Y. TANAKA,
    Vice-President,
    Japanese Confederation of Labour (DOMEI),
    c/o Zankadomei, Yukaikan 2-20-12,
    Minato-ku,
    TOKYO

    Mr. Y. YAMADA,
    Member of the Research Department,
    General Council of Trade Unions of Japan (SOHYO),
    Shiba Park,
    Minato-ku,
    TOKYO

KENYA

    Mr. J.G. MOLLO,
    Secretary General,
    Railway African Union (Kenya),
    P.O. Box 72029,
    NAIROBI

    Mr. J.I. OTHIENO,
    Permanent Secretary,
    Ministry of Labour,
    P.O. Box 40326,
    NAIROBI

    Mr. J.B.O. OMONDI,
    Assistant Labour Commissioner,
    Ministry of Labour,
    P.O. Box 40326,
    NAIROBI

LIBYA

    Mr. M. KADIKI,
    Member,
    Libya's Employers' Association,
    P.O. Box 1005,
    TRIPOLI

LUXEMBOURG

    M. R.A. SCHINTGEN,
    Conseiller de Gouvernement Adjoint,
    Ministère du Travail et de la Sécurité Sociale,
    57, bvd. de la Pétrusse,
    LUXEMBOURG

MADAGASCAR

    M. D. RAJAKOBA,
    Ministre de la Fonction Publique et du Travail,
    TANANARIVE

    M. N. RAKOTO,
    Directeur de Travail,
    Ministère de la Fonction Publique et du Travail,
    TANANARIVE

    M. S. RAKOTONDRAINIBE,
    Secrétaire Général du Syndicat des Industries de Madagascar,
    B.P. 2695,
    TANANARIVE

    M. G. RAKOTOARIMANGA,
    Secrétaire Général du syndicat Professional du Personnel
      autonome administratif de l'Université de Madagascar,
    TANANARIVE

MALAYSIA

Mr. J.H.H. HO,
Personnel Manager,
Fraser and Neave (M) Sdn. Bhd.,
Jalan Foss,
KUALA LUMPUR

Mr. J.D. KIRUBANATHAN,
Assistant Director of Industrial Relations,
Ministry of Labour and Manpower,
Jalan Raja K.2,
KUALA LUMPUR

Mr. A.H. PONNIAH,
Member of the Executive Council,
Malaysian Trade Union Congress,
42 Lorong Temenggong,
Off Jalan Cochrane,
KUALA LUMPUR

MAURITIUS

Mr. C. RAMBOCUS,
Senior Labour Officer,
Ministry of Labour and Industrial Relations,
Government House,
PORT LOUIS

MEXICO

Sr. J.E. DOMINGUEZ,
Director General de Programación y Encargado del despacho,
Instituto Nacional de Estudios del Trabajo,
MEXICO

NETHERLANDS

Mr. J. GROENENDAAL,
Director of Industrial Organisation,
  Works Councils and Property Acquisition,
Ministry of Social Affairs,
73, Zeestraat,
THE HAGUE

Miss C. HAK,
Head of the International Social Affairs Division,
Federation of Netherlands' Industry,
Postbox 2110,
THE HAGUE

Mr. J. DE JONG,
Secretary,
Federation of Netherlands' Industry,
Prinses Betrixlaan 5,
Postbus 2110,
THE HAGUE

Mr. H. THOMAS,
Senior Lecturer (Labour Economics) in the Labour
  Relations Programme,
Institute of Social Studies,
27, Molenstraat,
THE HAGUE

NIGERIA

Mr. N.N. AJAERO,
General Secretary,
Union of Posts and Telecommunications Technologists
  of Nigeria,
27, Montgomery Road,
YABA - LAGOS

Mr. M. AJOSE-ADEOGUN,
Personnel Director,
Shell Nigeria Ltd.,
Shell House,
Marina, LAGOS

Mr. C. EKPIKEN,
Personnel Manager,
UAC of Nigeria Limited,
Niger House,
P.O. Box 2058,
LAGOS

Mr. J.A. LIBINJO,
Assistant Director of Labour (Industrial Relations),
Federal Ministry of Labour,
Tafawa Balewa Square,
LAGOS

Mr. B.E. UKPABI,
Counsellor (Labour),
Permanent Mission of Nigeria,
44, rue de Lausanne,
1201 GENEVA (Switzerland)

NORWAY

Mr. B. BERNHARDSEN,
Ccunsellor,
Co-operation Council LO (Federation of Trade Unions),
  NAF (Norwegian Employers' Confederation),
Vika,
1552 OSLO 1

Mr. B. GUSTAVSEN,
Researcher,
The Work Research Institute,
Gydas v. 8,
OSLO 3

Mr. K. HALDEN,
Director-General,
Ministry of Local Government and Labour,
Pilestr. 33,
OSLO 1

Mr. S. HALVORSEN,
Solicitor,
Norwegian Federation of Trade Unions,
Ycungsgt. 11,
OSLO 1

Mr. Ø. SKARD,
Director of the Department of Management Development,
Norwegian Employers' Confederation,
P.B.6710, St. Olavs plass,
OSLO 1

PAKISTAN

Mr. K. AHMAD,
Secretary,
All Pakistan Federation of Trade Unions,
Labour Hall,
28 Nisbet Road,
LAHORE

Mr. G. HUSAIN,
Jcint Secretary,
Ministry of Labour and Works,
ISLAMABAD

Mr. S.A. HUSAIN,
Director (Technical),
Colony Textile Mills Ltd.,
PO ISMAILABAD Dist. Mutlan

PHILIPPINES

Mr. M.A. DIA,
Director,
Asian Labor Education Center (ALEC),
University of the Philippines,
QUEZON CITY

Mr. A.G. INCIONG,
Under Secretary of Labor,
Department of Labor,
MANILA

Mr. R.J. JABAR,
Executive Vice-President,
Federation of Free Workers,
Suite E, Ysmael Apts,
1845 Taft Avenue,
MANILA

Mr. R. OBEJAS,
Vice-President,
Philippine Transport General Workers' Organisation,
Port Area,
MANILA

POLAND

M. T. JAWORSKI,
Chef de la Section Socio-Professionnelle,
Conseil Central des Syndicats de Pologne,
ul. Kopernika 36/40,
00-328 WARSZAWA

SINGAPORE

Mr. K. MOK,
Head of General Management Unit,
National Productivity Board,
Off Corporation Road,
Jurong Town,
SINGAPORE 22

Mrs. G. OH,
Personnel Manager,
Union Carbide Singapore PTE Ltd.,
PO Box 42,
Bukit Panjang Post Office,
SINGAPORE 23

SPAIN

Sr. E. MANZANO GARCIA,
Presidente,
Consejo de Trabajadores de Guipuzcoa,
Marina 9 - 3º - izqda,
SAN SEBASTIAN

Sr. M. MOIX MARTINEZ,
Jefe de la Asesoría Técnica de Asuntos,
   Sociales Internacionales,
Ministerio de Trabajo,
Nuevos Ministerios,
Avda de Generalísimo,
MADRID

Sr. J.L. RIVERA Y SANCHEZ-CHAPARRO,
Jefe de la Sección de Normas Especiales de Industrias
   Textiles y de la Confección, Vestido y Tocado,
Ministerio de Trabajo,
Augustín de Bethancourt, 4,
MADRID

SRI_LANKA

Mr. G. JAYASURIYA,
Personnel Director,
Lever Brothers Limited,
258 Grandpass Road,
COLOMBO

Mr. W.L.P. DE MEL,
Commissioner of Labour,
Department of Labour,
PO Box 575,
COLOMBO

Mr. P. NAVARATNAM,
Deputy Commissioner of Labour (Industrial Relations),
Department of Labour,
COLOMBO 5

Mr. R. WEERAKOON,
General Secretary,
Ceylon Federation of Labour,
17/2 Kuruppu Road,
COLOMBO 8

SWEDEN

Mr. C. ASPLUND,
Ombudsman,
The Swedish Central Organization of Salaried Employees,
Box 5252,
S-102 STOCKHOLM

Mr. B. BRODEN,
Head of Section,
Ministry of Industry,
Fack,
S-103 10 - STOCKHOLM

Mr. L. GRAFSTRÖM,
Assistant Director,
Swedish Employers' Confederation,
Box 16 120,
S-103 23 STOCKHOLM 16

Mr. O. HAMMARSTRÖM,
Head of Section,
Ministry of Labour,
Fack,
S-103 10 STOCKHOLM

Mr. T.E. LIDBOM,
Secretary,
The Swedish Trade Union Confederation,
S-105 53 STOCKHOLM

Mr. J.-P. NORSTEDT,
Assistant Director,
Swedish Employers' Confederation,
Box 16 120,
S-103 STOCKHOLM 16

SWITZERLAND

M. J.-P. BONNY,
Directeur,
Office fédéral de l'Industrie, des Arts et Métiers
   et du Travail,
Bundesgasse 8,
3003 BERNE

M. G. NOBEL,
Secrétaire général,
Union Syndicale suisse,
Case Postale 64,
3000 BERNE 23

TANZANIA

Mr. O. JUMA,
Personnel and Public Relations Manager,
Kilimanjaro Textile Corporation Ltd.,
Dar es Salaam Mill,
P.O. Box 9164,
DAR ES SALAAM

Mr. A.P. KASANGA,
Senior Labour Office Grade I,
Ministry of Labour and Social Welfare,
P.O. Box 1181,
DAR ES SALAAM

Mr. B.L. SAGAWALLA,
Assistant Secretary General,
National Union of Tanganyika Workers,
P.O. Box 15359,
DAR ES SALAAM

TURKEY

Mr. T.Y. ERSOY,
Head of the Research Board,
Ministry of Labour,
Hosdere Caddesi No: 11/1,
Ayranci-ANKARA

Mr. G. TALAS,
Professor of Social Economy and Labour Law at the
   Faculty of Political Sciences,
University of Ankara,
Sehit Erzan Caddesi No: 34/15,
Cankaya, ANKARA

Mr. A. YOLUC,
Deputy Secretary-General,
Turkish Confederation of Employers' Associations,
Mithatpasa Caddesi 46/1,
Yenisshir-<u>ANKARA</u>

Mr. C. ZIYLAN,
Undersecretary,
Ministry of Labour,
Cetin Ziylan,
Cankaya, Abidin Daver Sokak ME-SA,
Sitesi C/18, <u>ANKARA</u>

<u>UNITED ARAB EMIRATES</u>

Mr. A.D. AHRAM,
Expert,
Ministry of Labour,
<u>ABU DHABI</u>

<u>UNITED KINGDOM</u>

Mr. J.L. EDWARDS,
Under Secretary Industrial Relations,
Department of Employment,
8 St. James's Square,
<u>LONDON</u> SW1

Mr. R.H. GILBERT,
Social Affairs Research Department,
Confederation of British Industry,
21 Tothill Street,
<u>LONDON</u> SW1

Mr. G. LLOYD,
Executive Member,
Union of Construction Allied Trades and Technicians,
Trades Union Congress,
Congress House,
Gt. Russell Street,
<u>LONDON</u> WC1B 3LS

<u>accompanied by</u>:   Mr. J. CANNEL,
                   Assistant Secretary,
                   Trades Union Congress,
                   Congress House,
                   <u>LONDON</u> WC1B 3LS

Mr. D. NAYLOR,
Head of Employee Relations,
Shell International Petroleum Company Ltd.,
Shell Centre,
<u>LONDON</u> SE1 7NA

Mr. T.B. OWEN,
Company Personnel Manager,
Imperial Chemical Industries Ltd.,
I.C. House,
Millbank,
LONDON SW1

UNITED STATES OF AMERICA

Mr. R. BOOTH,
Labor Attaché,
American Embassy,
OSLO

Mr. B. MILLEN,
Office of the Assistant Secretary for Policy,
   Evaluation and Research,
US Department of Labor, Room 5119,
WASHINGTON, D.C. 20210

Mr. P.F. SHAW,
Vice-President,
Chase Manhattan Bank,
One Chase Manhattan Plaza,
NEW YORK, New York 10015

Mr. B. SOFFER,
Labor Economist,
Bureau of Domestic Commerce (Room 3108),
US Department of Commerce,
WASHINGTON, D.C. 20230

Mr. P.J. WEINBERG,
Director of Employee Relations,
American Express Company,
770 Broadway,
NEW YORK CITY, 10003

Mr. W. WINPISINGER,
General Vice-President,
International Association of Machinists and
   Aerospace Workers,
1300 Connecticut Avenue, N.W.,
WASHINGTON, D.C. 20036

USSR

Mr. R.A. GRIGORJAN,
Chief of Section of the International Department,
All-Union Central Council of Trade Unions of the USSR,
Leninskii prospekt 42,
MOSCOW 5-119

Mr. V.I. MARKOV,
Chief of Section at the Research Institute of Labour,
State Committee of Labour and Wages,
Pl. Koujbysheva 1,
MOSCOW K-12

VENEZUELA

     Sr. J. MATOS ROMERO,
     Secretario General,
     Sindicato Petrolero del Distrito Federal y Edo Miranda,
     Calle Los Abogados,
     Qta. Alju. Los Chaguaramos,
     CARACAS

     Sr. P.R. AREVALO TRUJILLO,
     Assessor,
     Federación Venezolana de Camaras y Asociaciones de
       Comercio y Producción,
     Edificio Fedecamaras,
     Urbanización el Bosque,
     CARACAS

     Sr. Carlos LANDER MARQUEZ,
     Director,
     Creole Petroleum Corporation,
     CARACAS

VIET-NAM, REPUBLIC OF

     M. TRAN-HUU-QUYEN,
     Secrétaire général,
     Confédération Viêtnamienne du Travail,
     14, Lê-van-Duyêt,
     SAIGON

     M. TRUONG KHAC HUE,
     Secrétaire général,
     Confédération générale de l'Industrie et de
       l'Artisanat du Viêtnam,
     51, bên Chuong Duong,
     SAIGON 2

YUGOSLAVIA

     Mr. S. GROZDANIC,
     Professor at the Faculty of Political Sciences,
     University of Belgrade,
     Bulevar J.N.A. 45,
     11000 BELGRADE

     Mr. B. KAVCIC,
     Director of the Centre for Research on Self-Management,
     Republic Council of Federation of Trade Unions of Slovenia,
     Dalmatinova 4,
     LJUBLJANA

     Mr. N. PASIC,
     Professor at the Faculty of Political Sciences,
     University of Belgrade,
     Member of the Presidency of the Socialist Republic
       of Serbia,
     Proleterskih Brigada 31/I,
     11000 BELGRADE

Mr. M. ZUVELA,
Deputy Chairman of Trade Union Branch,
Shipyard "SPLIT",
Brodogradiliste "SPLIT",
SPLIT

ZAMBIA

Mr. U.C. CHISHIMBA,
Assistant Personnel Manager,
Nchanga Consolidated Copper Mines, Ltd.,
Anglo American Corporation,
P.O.Box 1986,
LUSAKA

Mr. J.K. KABASO,
Depot Supervisor,
Mining Timbers, Ltd.,
P.O.Box 1491,
KITWE

Mr. M.J. MVULA,
Area Personnel Manager (North),
Zambia Electricity Supply Corporation, Ltd.,
P.O.Box 1334,
NDOLA

Mr. NYIRENDA,
Principal,
The Ministry of Labour and Social Services,
P.O.Box 2186,
LUSAKA

Mr. G. SIBAJENE,
Group Industrial Relations Officer,
Industrial Development Corporation (INDECO) Limited,
P.O.Box 1935,
LUSAKA

Mr. M.K. SUMANI,
Regional Secretary,
Mineworkers' Union of Zambia,
P.O.Box 448,
KITWE

INTERNATIONAL CENTRE FOR ADVANCED TECHNICAL
AND VOCATIONAL TRAINING

Mr. J.L. BURBIDGE,
Professor,
International Centre for Advanced Technical and
   Vocational Training,
Corso Unità d'Italia, 140,
TURIN (Italy)

OBSERVERS

I. NORWAY

Mr. L. BJORHEIM,
Director,
Cooperation Council,
LO (Norwegian Federation of Trade Unions),
  NAF (Norwegian Employers' Confederation),
1552 Vika,
OSLO 1

Mr. A. ESKILD,
Deputy Director,
Ministry of Local Government and Labour,
Pilestr. 33,
OSLO 1

Mr. H.O. HANSEN,
Secretary,
Federation of Trade Unions,
Youngsgt. 11,
OSLO 1

Mr. K. HANSEN,
Head of Department of Productivity,
Norwegian Employers' Confederation,
P.B. 6710, St. Olavs plass,
OSLO 1

Mr. B. HAUG,
Attorney-General,
Chairman of the Commission on Industrial Democracy,
c/o Ministry of Local Government and Labour,
Pilestr. 33,
OSLO 1

Mr. H. HELDAL,
Chairman of the Norwegian ILO-Committee,
Royal Norwegian Ministry of Social Affairs,
Akersgt. 42, Oslo-Dep.,
OSLO 1

Mr. E. HOFF, M.B.A.,
Head of the International Office,
Norwegian Employers' Confederation,
P.B. 6710, St. Olavs plass,
OSLO 1

Mr. P. KRABY,
Director,
Norwegian Employers' Confederation,
P.B. 6710, St. Olavs plass,
OSLO 1

Mr. T. RØSSUM,
Managing Director,
A/S Nationaltrykkeriet and Forlagesbokbinderiet,
c/o The Norwegian Employers' Confederation,
P.B. 6710, St. Olavs plass,
OSLO 1

Mr. R. WEBSTER,
Chief of Division,
Ministry of Local Government and Labour,
Pilestr. 33,
OSLO 1

II. INTERNATIONAL ORGANISATIONS

ASIAN PRODUCTIVITY ORGANISATION

Mr. T.A. SUZUKI,
Industry Programme Officer,
Asian Productivity Organisation,
Aoyama Dai-ichi Mansions,
4-14 Akasaka 8-chome,
Minato-ku,
TOKYO 107 (Japan)

COUNCIL OF EUROPE

Mr. S. STRAY,
Vice-President of the Storting (Norwegian Parliament),
Stortinget,
OSLO 1 (Norway)

EUROPEAN COMMUNITIES

M. I.L. ROBERTS,
Administrateur Principal,
Commission des Communautés européenes,
Rue de la Loi, 200,
B-1040 BRUXELLES (Belgique)

M. K.M. SCHILTZ,
Administrateur Principal à la Direction Générale
   des Affaires Sociales,
Commission des Communautés européennes,
B-1040 BRUXELLES (Belgique)

ORGANISATION FOR ECONOMIC CO-OPERATION
AND DEVELOPMENT

Mr. R.O. CLARKE,
Principal Administrator at the Directorate for Social,
   Manpower and Education Affairs,
Organisation for Economic Co-operation and Development,
2, rue André-Pascal,
75775 PARIS CEDEX 16 (France)

INTERNATIONAL_CONFEDERATION_OF
FREE_TRADE_UNIONS

    Mr. P. COLDRICK,
    Secretary of Economic and Social Committee,
    International Confederation of Free Trade Unions,
    Rue Montagne aux Herbes Potagères, 37-41,
    B-1000 BRUXELLES (Belgique)

INTERNATIONAL_ORGANISATION_OF_EMPLOYERS

    Mr. G. BERGENSTRÖM,
    President,
    International Organisation of Employers,
    Svenska Arbetsgivareföreningen,
    P.O.Box 16 120,
    S-103 23 STOCKHOLM 16 (Sweden)

    Mr. A. BEATON,
    Manager of the Industrial Division,
    Chamber of Commerce and Industry of South Australia,
    Industry House,
    12 Pirie House,
    ADELAIDE, South Australia, 5000

    Mr. C. CASTLE,
    British Petroleum Company, Ltd.,
    Moor Lane,
    LONDON EC2 (UK)

    Mlle C. DE BLOCK,
    Assistante du Secrétaire général,
    Organisation Internationale des Employeurs,
    98, rue de Saint-Jean,
    1201 GENEVE (Suisse)

    M. J.-J. OECHSLIN,
    Chef du Service des relations avec l'OIT,
    Conseil National du Patronat Français,
    31, avenue Pierre 1er de Serbie,
    F - 75784 PARIS CEDEX 16 (France)

    M. J.R.E. PORIER,
    Chargé des questions de relation du personnel en Europe,
    Shell International,
    Karel van Bylandtlaan 30,
    LA HAYE (Pays-Bas)

WORLD_FEDERATION_OF_TRADE_UNIONS

    M. C. DE ANGELI,
    Représentant permanent de la FSM auprès de l'ONU
      et du BIT à Genève,
    10 rue Fendt,
    1201 GENEVE (Suisse)

NORWEGIAN TRIPARTITE ORGANISING COMMITTEE

Chairman:

Mr. Østein Opdahl   Counsellor, Royal Norwegian
Ministry of Social Affairs.

Members:

Mr. H.O. Hansen   Secretary, The Norwegian Federation
of Trade Unions (LO).

Mr. P. Kraby   Director, the Norwegian Employers'
Confederation (NAF).

Mr. H. Webster   Chief of Division, Ministry of Local
Government and Labour.

Secretary:

Mr. Bjarne Flølo   Royal Norwegian Ministry of Social
Affairs.

NORWEGIAN SECRETARIAT

Miss Solveig Petterson   Royal Norwegian Ministry of Social
Affairs.

Mr. Arne Lie   Ministry of Local Government and
Labour.

Mr. Paal Olav Berg   Ministry of Local Government and
Labour.

Mr. Hakon Cordt Hansen   Ministry of Local Government and
Labour.

Mr. Lars Chr. Berge   Norwegian Employers' Confederation.

Mr. Per Myklebost   Norwegian Employers' Confederation.

Miss Mirjam Nordahl   Norwegian Federation of Trade Unions.

Mrs. Susi Ochsenbein   Norwegian Federation of Trade Unions.

Mr. Kjell Skovholt

Mr. Joep Bolweg

ILO SECRETARIAT

Mr. Jean de Givry   Chairman of the Symposium

Mr. Johannes Schregle
Mr. Lengvard Khitrov
Mr. Jacques Monat
Mrs. Edythe Epstein
Mr. Alfred Pankert
Miss Evelyne Thulborn
Miss Jeanne Melloni

APPENDIX IV

LIST OF WRITTEN CONTRIBUTIONS

The following documents are obtainable on request to the Labour Law and Labour Relations Branch, International Labour Office, Geneva.

The missing numbers (1, 26, 67, 75, 82) have either been reproduced above or concerned the material arrangements for the Symposium and are no longer of any interest.

(E = English, F = French, S = Spanish)

Number	Author and title	Language
2	Mr. Karl Fitting: Workers' participation in decisions within undertakings in the Federal Republic of Germany	E,F,S
3	Mr. N.M. Vakil and Mr. S. Aggarwal: Workers' participation in management in India, A practical approach	E,F,S
4	Miss C. Hak and Mr. J. de Jong: Workers' participation in decisions within undertakings in the Netherlands	E,F,S
5	Mr. J.B. Hounongbe: Workers' participation in decisions within undertakings in Dahomey	E,F,S
6	Mr. B. Hardmeier: The Swiss trade unions and participation (Switzerland)	E,F,S
7	Mr. E. Manzano García: Workers and the exercise of power within the undertaking (Spain)	E,F,S
8	Mr. C. Asplund, Mr. L. Grafström, Mr. O. Hammarström and Mr. T.E. Lidbom: Workers' participation in decisions within undertakings in Sweden	E,F,S
9	Mr. J.P. Norstedt: The new working life - Experience from the shop-floor level in Swedish industry	E,F,S
10	Mr. J. Groenendaal: Workers' participation in decisions within undertakings in the Netherlands	E,F,S
11	Mr. D. DeNorre, Workers' participation in decisions within undertakings in Belgium	E,F,S

Number	Author and title	Language
12	Mr. W.L.P. de Mel: Workers' participation in decisions within under- takings in Sri_Lanka	E,F,S
13	Mr. R. Weerakoon: Employees' councils in Sri_Lanka and the next step forward	E,F,S
14	The Ministry of Local Government and Labour, the Norwegian Employers' Confederation, and Mr. Thoralf Ulrik Quale, Work Research Institute, Oslo: Workers' participation in decisions within under- takings in Norway	E,F,S
15	Mr. J. Gayetot: Workers' participation in decisions within under- takings in Belgium	E,F,S
16	Mr. K. Herczeg: Workers' participation in decisions within under- takings in Hungary	E,F,S
17	Dr. N. Pasic: Socialism in Yugoslavia. Theory and practice. Transformation of self-management in Yugoslavia into an integral, economic and political system	E,F,S
18	Mr. J.P. Bonny: Workers' participation in decisions within under- takings in Switzerland	E,F,S
19	Mr. J. Ribadeau Dumas: A concerted approach between management and super- visory staff in France	E,F,S
20	Mr. J.L. Rivera y Sánchez-Chaparro: La participación de los trabajadores in las decisiones dentro de la empresa en España	S
21	Mr. E.M. Parchment: Workers' participation in decisions within under- takings in Jamaica	E
22	Mr. J. Ho Hwa Hiong, Mr. A.H. Ponniah and Mr. J.D. Kirubanathan: Workers' participation in decisions within under- takings in Malaysia	E
23	Mr. M.S. Krishnan: Workers' participation in decisions within under- takings in India	E
24	Mr. M. Salmonperä, Miss T. Halonen, Mr. H. Joustie, Mr. T. Saukkonen: Workers' participation in decisions within under- takings in Finland	E

Number	Author and title	Language
25	Mr. S.D. Al-Bayatti: Workers' participation in decisions within under- takings in Iraq	E
27	Mr. G. Heinrich and Mr. M. Mayer: Workers' participation in decisions within under- takings in Austria	E
28	Mr. M.S.S. Varadan: Workers' participation in decisions within under- takings in India	E
29	Mr. C. Rambocus: Workers' participation in decisions within under- takings in Mauritius	E
30	Miss M.E. Kenrick: Workers' participation in decisions within under- takings in Jamaica	E
31	Mr. K. Mok: Works councils in Singapore	E
32	Mr. M.R. Chowdhury: Workers' participation in decisions within under- takings in Bangladesh	E
33	Mr. H. Ronnenberg: Workers' participation in decisions within under- takings in the Federal Republic of Germany	E
34	Mr. O. Juma: Workers' participation in decisions within under- takings in Tanzania	E
35	Mrs. G. Oh: Workers' participation in decisions within under- takings in Singapore	E
36	Mr. N.N. Ajaero: Workers' participation in decisions within under- takings in Nigeria	F
37	Mr. M.G. Mortuja: Workers' participation in decisions within under- takings in Bangladesh	E
38	Mrs. Azra Ali: Workers' participation in decisions within under- takings in Bangladesh	E
39	Mr. J. Chazal: La participation des travailleurs aux décisions dans l'entreprise en France	F
40	Mr. B.E. Ukpabi: Workers' participation in decisions within under- takings in Nigeria	E

Number	Author and title	Language
41	Mr. T. Shiraishi: Workers' participation in decisions within under-takings in <u>Japan</u>	E
42	Mr. R. Jabar: Workers' participation in decisions within under-takings in the <u>Philippines</u>	E
43	Mr. M. Nair: Workers' participation in decisions within under-takings in <u>India</u>	E
44	Professor John J. Burbidge: The effect of group production methods on workers' participation in decisions (International Centre for Advanced Technical and Vocational Training - Turin)	E
45	Mr. B. Bordrup and Mr. P. Roose: Industrial democracy in <u>Denmark</u>	E
46	Mr. C. Ekpiken: Workers' participation in decisions within under-takings in <u>Nigeria</u>	E
47	Mr. R. Schintgen: La participation des travailleurs aux décisions dans l'entreprise au Grand-Duché de <u>Luxembourg</u>	F
48	Mr. K. Ahmad: Workers' participation in decisions within under-takings in <u>Pakistan</u>	E
49	Mr. G. Lloyd and Mr. J. Cannell: Workers' participation in decisions within under-takings in the <u>United Kingdom</u>	E
50	Mr. J.A. Labinjo: Workers' participation in decisions within under-takings in <u>Nigeria</u>	E
51	Mr. U.C. Chishimba: Workers' participation in decisions within under-takings in <u>Zambia</u>	E
52	Mr. Ghulam Husain: Workers' participation in decisions within under-takings in <u>Pakistan</u>	E
53	Mr. Y. Tanaka: Workers' participation in decisions within under-takings in <u>Japan</u>	E
54	Mr. Francisco Matos Romero: La participación de los trabajadores en las decisiones dentro de la empresa en <u>Venezuela</u>	S

Number	Author and title	Language
55	Mr. R. De Buck: La participation des travailleurs aux décisions dans l'entreprise en <u>Belgique</u>	F
56	Mr. L. Chavrot: La participation et les droits des travailleurs à l'information, à la négociation et au contrôle dans les entreprises (<u>France</u>)	F
57	Mr. G.H. Webb: Participation - Myth or reality (<u>United Kingdom</u>)	E
58	Mr. N.N. Chatterjee: The Government's role in promoting workers' participation in <u>India</u>	E
59	Mr. M.E. Palladin: La participation des travailleurs aux décisions dans l'entreprise en <u>Italie</u>	F
60	Mr. G. Forlenza: La participation des travailleurs aux décisions dans les entreprises en <u>Italie</u>	F
61	Mr. C. Talas: La participation des travailleurs aux décisions dans les entreprises en <u>Turquie</u>	F
62	Mr. T. Naruse: Workers' participation in decisions within under- takings in <u>Japan</u>	E
63	Mr. Mladen Zuvela: The structure of management in the organisation of associated work (example is the shipyard "Split") (<u>Yugoslavia</u>)	E
64	Mr. Reinhard Sommer: Some aspects regarding the involvement of the working class and its trade unions in planning and managing national economy in the <u>German Democratic Republic</u>	E
65	Dr. Bogdan Kavcic: Workers' participation in decisions within under- takings in <u>Yugoslavia</u>	E
66	Mr. G. Sibajene, Mr. J.K. Kabaso and Mr. M. Mvula: Workers' participation in decisions within under- takings in <u>Zambia</u>	E
68	Mr. Osvaldo H. Vilas Figallo: La participación de los trabajadores en una empresa de servicios públicos. Informe sobre el proceso de autogestión en SEGBA (<u>Argentina</u>)	S
69	Mr. S.S. Grozdanic: Workers' self-management and foreign investments in <u>Yugoslavia</u>	E

Number	Author and title	Language
70	Mr. Truong-Khac-Hue: La participation des travailleurs aux décisions dans l'entreprise en Républic du Viet-Nam	F
71	Mr. M.A. Chérief: La participation des travailleurs aux décisions dans l'entreprise en Algérie	F
72	Mr. P. Guillen: Note sur les démarches et expériences mettant en place dans les ateliers des arrangements en vue d'associer les travailleurs à l'organisation du travail en France	F
73	Mr. J.A.J. Caine: Workers' participation in decisions within undertakings in Australia	E
74	Mr. T. Jaworski: Workers' participation in decisions within undertakings in Poland	E
76	Mr. G. Arrigo: Le mouvement syndical italien et la participation (Italie)	F
77	Mr. H. Thomas: Economic theory and "economic democracy" (the Netherlands)	E
78	Mr. Karl-Heinz Janzen: The collective agreement as an instrument of trade union action to safeguard workers' interests (Federal Republic of Germany)	E
79	Mr. V.I. Markov: Socialist emulation as a form of enlisting the working people in the management of production in the USSR	E
80	Mr. R.A. Grigorjan: The role and activities of the trade unions of the USSR in drawing the working people into the planning and management of production	E
81	Mr. S. Rakotondrainibe: La participation des travailleurs aux décisions dans les entreprises à Madagascar	F

OTHER ISSUES IN THE LABOUR-MANAGEMENT
RELATIONS SERIES

No. 1. The role of government in the field of labour-management relations - Canadian approach (Geneva, 1957), out of print.

No. 2. Two examples of practical action to improve labour-management relations:

(1)   Peru - July-August 1957, and

(2)   Bolivia - October 1957 (Geneva, 1957), out of print.

No. 3. Some aspects of labour-management relations in Asia (Geneva, 1958), out of print.

No. 4. International standards and guiding principles 1944-58 (Geneva, 1958). This issue has been amalgamated with No. 14 and brought up to date in No. 24.

No. 5. Workers' management and labour relations in Yugoslavia (Geneva, 1959), out of print.

No. 6. An account of an Asian bipartite study tour on labour-management relations to the United Kingdom and Federal Republic of Germany - 6 September-8 November 1958 (Geneva, 1959).

No. 7. The position and responsibilities of the personnel department inside undertakings (Geneva, 1960), out of print.

No. 8. Status and duties of workers' representatives (Geneva, 1960).

No. 9. Report to the Government of India on labour-management relations and some aspects of wages policy (Geneva, 1960), out of print.

No. 10. Reports on the visit of a joint team of experts on labour-management relations to Pakistan and Ceylon (Geneva, 1961), out of print.

No. 11. Some aspects of labour-management relations in the American region: A summary of the discussions of the Inter-American Study Conference on Labour-Management Relations, Montevideo, 3-12 November 1960 (Geneva, 1961).

No. 11(a). Some aspects of labour-management relations in the American region: Reports prepared by the International Labour Office for the Inter-American Study Conference on Labour-Management Relations, Montevideo, 3-12 November 1960 (Geneva, 1962).

No. 12. Personnel relations in a growing enterprise: A case study of an Israeli undertaking (Geneva, 1962).

No. 13. Consultations and co-operation between employers and workers at the level of the enterprise: Outline of the regulations in force in eleven European countries - Report drawn up in collaboration with the OECD (Geneva, 1962).

No. 14. International standards and guiding principles 1958-61 (Geneva, 1962), out of print; new edition brought up to date published under No. 44.

No. 15. Prevention and settlement of industrial disputes in Asia - Documents submitted to and report of an Asian Regional Seminar, Kuala Lumpur, 7-19 December 1961 (Geneva, 1962).

No. 16. Government services for the improvement of labour-managenent relations and settlement of disputes in Asia - An account of the work of the Labour-Management Relations Committee, Fifth Asian Regional Conference, Melbourne, 1962 (Geneva, 1963).

No. 17. Basic agreements and joint statements on labour-management relations (Geneva, 1963).

No. 18. Report to the Government of India on the organisation and development of a government personnel management advisory service (Geneva, 1963).

No. 19. Report to the Government of Turkey on the visit of a joint mission of experts on labour-management relations (18 November-15 December 1962) (Geneva, 1963).

No. 20. The role of labour ministries in the improvement of labour-management relations in Latin America (Geneva, 1964), out of print.

No. 21. Scope and methods of collective bargaining in the iron and steel industry. Report submitted to and proceedings of the Seventh Session of the Iron and Steel Committee, Cardiff, 26 August-6 September 1963 (Geneva, 1964).

No. 22. Industrial relations in certain African countries - Documentation and summary of proceedings of a Seminar on Industrial Relations, Abidjan, 15-26 October 1963 (Geneva, 1964), out of print.

No. 23. Reports to the Government of Ceylon on labour-management relations training and on labour-management relations and personnel management at the Gal Oya Development Board (Geneva, 1964).

No. 24. International standards and guiding principles, 1944-64 (Geneva, 1965), cut of print; new edition brought up to date published under No. 44.

No. 25. Certain aspects of labour-management relations within the undertaking - Documents of a technical meeting, Geneva, 5-14 October 1964 (Geneva, 1965).

No. 26. Institutional aspects of labour-management relations inside undertakings in Asia - Record of proceedings of and contributions submitted to an Asian Regional Seminar, Kandy, 19-30 April 1965 (Geneva, 1966).

No. 27. The role of employers' and workers' organisations in programming and planning in the metal trades: Report submitted to and proceedings of the Eighth Session of the Metal Trades Committee, Geneva, 6-17 December 1965 (Geneva, 1967).

No. 28. Practical measures to promote good labour-management relations on plantations: Report submitted to and proceedings of the Fifth Session of the Committee on Work on Plantations, Geneva, 2-13 May 1966 (Geneva, 1967).

No. 29. Methods of collective bargaining and settlements of disputes in rail transport: Report submitted to and proceedings of the Eighth Session of the Inland Transport Committee, Geneva, 21 November-2 December 1966 (Geneva, 1967).

No. 30. Informe al Gobierno de la República del Perú sobre la mediación y conciliación de los conflictos colectivos de trabajo (Ginebra, 1968), only in Spanish.

No. 31. . Labour-management relations in public industrial undertakings in Asia: Report submitted to and proceedings of the 13th Session of the Asian Advisory Committee, Singapore, November-December 1966 (Geneva, 1968), out of print.

No. 32. Rights of trade union representatives at the level of the undertaking: Documents of a technical meeting, Geneva, 20-29 November 1967 (Geneva, 1969).

No. 33. Participation of workers in decisions within under-takings: Documents of a technical meeting, Geneva, 20-29 November 1967 (Geneva, 1969).

No. 34. International standards and guiding principles, 1944-68 (Geneva, 1969), cut of print; new edition brought up to date published under No. 44.

No. 35. Management development and personnel policies and practices in Asia: An account of the work of the Management Development Committee, Sixth Asian Regional Conference, Tokyo, 1968 (Geneva, 1969), out of print.

No. 36. The role of employers' and workers' organisations in programming and planning in the iron and steel industry: Report submitted to and proceedings of the Eighth Session of the Iron and Steel Committee, Geneva, 29 September-9 October 1969 (Geneva, 1970).

No. 37. Conciliation and arbitration of industrial disputes in English-speaking countries of Africa: Record of proceedings of and contributions submitted to an African Regional Seminar, Kampala, November 1969 (Geneva, 1970).

No. 38. Basic agreements and joint statements on labour-management relations (Geneva, 1971).

No. 39. Role of employers' organisations in Asian countries: Record of proceedings and documents submitted to an Asian Round Table, Tokyo, December 1970 (Geneva, 1971).

No. 40. Industrial relations and personnel management in English-speaking Africa: Record of proceedings of and documents submitted to a seminar, Dar es Salaam, October-November 1971 (Geneva, 1972).

No. 41. Freedom of association for workers' and employers' organisations and their role in social and economic development: An account of the work of the Committee on Workers' and Employers' Organisations, Seventh Asian Regional Conference, Teheran, 1971 (Geneva, 1972).

No. 42. Role of employers' organisations in English-speaking African countries: Record of proceedings of and documents submitted to an African Round Table, Addis Ababa, October 1972 (Geneva, 1973).

No. 43. Labour relations in the Caribbean region: Record of proceedings of and documents submitted to a Caribbean Regional Seminar on Labour Relations, Port-of-Spain, March 1973 (Geneva, 1973).

No. 44. International standards and guiding principles, 1944-73 (Geneva, 1974).

No. 45. Social problems of contract, subcontract and casual labour in the petroleum industry: Report submitted to and proceedings of the Eighth Session of the Petroleum Committee, Geneva, April 1973 (Geneva, 1974).

No. 46. Rôle des organisations d'employeurs dans les pays d'Afrique francophone. Compte rendu des travaux d'une table ronde africaine, Abidjan, March-April 1974 (Geneva, 1975). In French only.

No. 47. Employers' organisations and industrial relations in Asia: Record of proceedings of and documents submitted to a Regional Technical Seminar, Jakarta, November 1974 (Geneva, 1975).